The Century of
Hats

The Century of Hats

Headturning Style of the Twentieth Century

SUSIE HOPKINS

AURUM

To Mutti,
who was my inspiration, and to Rhys, Annelies,
and Fiona who grew up with hats.
With love

A QUINTET BOOK

First published in Great Britain
1999 by Aurum Press Ltd
25 Bedford Avenue, London WC1B 3AT

A catalogue record for this book is available from the British Library.

ISBN 1-85410-662-7

1 3 5 7 9 10 8 6 4 2
1999 2001 2003 2002 2000

This book was designed and produced by
Quintet Publishing Limited
6 Blundell Street
London N7 9BH

Creative Director: Richard Dewing
Art Director: Paula Marchant
Project Editor: Debbie Foy
Designer: Caroline Grimshaw

Typeset in Great Britain by
Central Southern Typesetters, Eastbourne
Manufactured in Hong Kong by
Regent Publishing Services Ltd
Printed in China by
Leefung-Asco Printers Ltd

ACKNOWLEDGMENTS

My thanks must go to the friends who encouraged me to write this book; to my editor, Debbie Foy, for her guidance and support; and to Cal McCrystal for his help and advice.
I would also like to thank all the milliners in New York, London, and Paris for their time and for their continued enthusiasm and love of hats.

PHOTOGRAPHIC CREDITS

Ketchum Life (Max Factor/Dolmio): 2, 142, 143; **Lanvin**: 7, 26, 39, 42, 44, 45; **Herald & Heart Hatters, London**: 8, 9, 145; **Harry Abrams**, New York: 11; **Hulton-Getty**: 12, 13, 14, 18, 19, 20, 25, 27, 28, 30, 36, 37, 41, 47, 49, 58, 61, 65, 68, 69, 74, 77, 83, 89, 91, 97, 102, 104, 109, 113, 120, 155; **ET Archive**: 15, 16, 21, 32, 95; **Advertising Archives**: 18, 23, 38, 63, 107, 121, 134; **Pepin Press**: 19, 43, 46; **Condé Nast Publications**: 19, 24, 26, 29, 31, 36, 39, 46, 86, 98, 99, 112; **Musée du Chapeau**: 21, 154; **Patou**: 28, 40, 41; **Fashion Institute of Technology**, New York: 29; **Mr Ronnie Barker**: 29, 43, 60; **Chanel Archives**: 30; **Lock and Co. Hatmakers**: 32, 33, 48, 94, 116, 117, 120, 121; **Pamela Lee**: 33; **Vintage Magazine Archive**: 35, 51, 52, 55, 56, 57, 59, 61, 71, 87, 90, 93, 103, 128; **Pictorial Press**: 48, 53, 70, 84, 85, 95; **Musée de la Mode et du Textile, Paris**: 58; **Aquarius Pictures**: 62, 63, 81, 100; **Ulrike Koëb, Vienna**: 66, 72, 73, 75; **Christian Dior**: 76, 142; **Luton Museum**: 78, 79; **Editions du Rouergue**: 80; **Fiona Tromans**: 88, 137; **Jean Barthet**: 101, 103, 105, 106; **Stephen Jones**: 123; **Lacroix**: 124; **Tim Graham Picture Library**: 125, 126, 127; **Robert Fairer**: 138, 139, 156, 157; **Bill Horsman, Worshipful Company of Feltmakers**: 129; **Info Plan (Perrier)**: 142

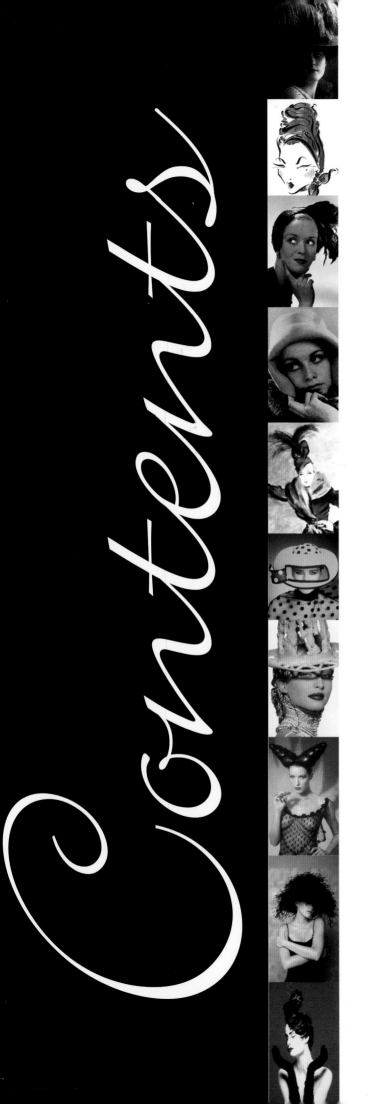

Contents

Foreword

FROM THE ICE AGE, AND THROUGHOUT HISTORY, MAN HAS COVERED and adorned his head. First, headgear was a form of protection from the elements, but hats in all their different styles became an expression of status, tradition, and style and have played an important role in social history and in the life of the twentieth century.

During this century, hats have shown much diversity and milliners have expressed their creativity in adapting designs to the spirit of the time and the fashion. Chanel, one of the most famous names in fashion, was a milliner before she built her *couture* empire, and a forerunner of the great Parisian millinery tradition in the first half of this century.

In my lifetime, Aage Thaarup, in London, was a master of his art and I treasure the picture of the young Queen Elizabeth II riding side-saddle wearing his hat. Halston in New York, who created Jackie Kennedy's pillbox hat, was not only a fine milliner, but developed into an American *couturier* of high standing. I admired Jean Barthet and the charming Madame Paulette in Paris, with whom I worked closely in the Sixties and Seventies.

There are so many names, both of the past and the present, featured in this book. It will be most enjoyable to dwell in the memory of hats in this century and the book will be a reference for young milliners starting up, wherever in the world they may be. The future of hats will lay in their hands—or heads!

Philip Somerville

MILLINER AND WARRANT HOLDER TO
HER MAJESTY, QUEEN ELIZABETH II

Hats: Protection, Status, or Vanity?

Hats are *the* fashion accessories of the century. In all their different styles, moods, and guises they mirror the social and political changes of the last hundred years. Passionately loved by some, hats are dismissed as "old hat" by others. People keep secrets "under their hats," make decisions "at the drop of a hat," and pull tricks "out of a hat." "*Chapeau*" is a cry of admiration in France and its English equivalent "I take my hat off to you" is a great compliment. Hats are often admired and may be ridiculed or hotly debated, but they are always remembered.

Protection from the elements, falling objects, or injury are the fundamental reasons for headgear. As part of a uniform, a hat can be a sign of power and status, but can also signify belonging to a group, or stand out with a revolutionary spirit. Hats can be an expression of hierarchy, show professional status, reflect social distinctions and events, or mark traditional rites of passage at weddings and funerals.

In a fashion context, a hat is the most important accessory, because it has the power to enhance or destroy an image. It can frame or overshadow a face, enhance the eyes, and help to instill an air of power and aggression. Fashion historian James Laver observed that: "The whole region of the head is charged with unconscious significance, so that even today a respectable bank manager, by putting a paper hat on his head, can transform himself into a funny, irresponsible creature." He sums up his theory by suggesting, "The very moods of our souls are bound up with the kind of headgear we choose or do not choose."

The craft of millinery is only about 300 years old, although hatmakers, or *chapeliers*, in France have been around for much longer. The word "milliner," meaning fancy hatmakers in the United States and in Britain, has its origins in the seventeenth century. Merchants from Milan, Italy, called "Millaners" traveled across Europe with all kinds of finery, straws, and haberdashery. They sold their wares at the royal courts along the way and eventually settled and made hats in England. In France, the correct title for a person making hats for women is *modiste*, which is broadly similar to the German word *Modistin*.

The very first *grande modiste* was Rose Bertin, milliner and dress adviser to Queen Marie-Antoinette. Rose Bertin was responsible for elevating the role of dressmaker to that of a fashion designer and creator. The historical difference between hatmakers and milliners, still valid today, is that one makes hats for men, while the other makes them for women. This differential is blurring a little in today's unisex fashion age, and while it has historical basis, it might not be politically correct for much longer.

The work of milliners is subdivided into designers, model milliners, copyists, machinists, and trimmers. The correct title depends on a person's ability, what type of business they are working in, and on the kind of hats they are making. Modern millinery requires flexible people who can do everything, including packing hats, cleaning up, and running errands.

A model hat, however, is very different from a factory-produced hat even if it is a high-quality one, trimmed and finished by hand. The process of making a model hat means that one pair of hands **blocks**, constructs, and finishes the hat. A factory-produced hat is usually machine-blocked on hydraulic metal **pans**, and goes through various stages of machining and finishing along a production line.

Even the professional vocabulary of model milliners and millinery factories

⫿ Traditional millinery hat blocks handcarved from seasoned lime wood are becoming collectors' items today

varies. Ways of describing certain materials and professional expressions are subtle indications in differences the kind of millinery "upbringing" a person has received.

All hats—whether high-class models or a mass-produced ready-to-wear— go through a first stage of blocking or shaping of the raw material. It may be a fur or wool **felt hood**, a finely woven or plaited straw, or a foundation material to be covered with fabric. For speed hat factories work with metal blocking machines, while model milliners steam and shape hats individually on wooden or **sparterie** blocks. Sparterie

blocks are handmade hat shapes, which are reinforced and stiffened with **spartalac**. Sculpting the shapes is an art in itself, mastered by few millinery businesses today.

The material is shaped to the block with the help of steam, water, and hot irons. The edges of **crowns** and **brims** are secured with pins and **blocking cords**, and the blocked hat is put in a drying cupboard called an "oven" to dry. **Stiffening**—applied either before or after blocking—plays an important role and can be quite a delicate operation. In the nineteenth century, a toxic mercury mixture used to treat felt had harmful effects

▮ Flowers, feathers, and finery used for hat decorations

on workers in the industry. This was the origin of the expression "as mad as a hatter" and the inspiration for the character of the Hatter in *Alice's Adventures in Wonderland*. Modern stiffeners in use today are quite safe, but milliners and hatters may sometimes seem almost as eccentric as the one in Lewis Carroll's story.

When the blocked straw or felt shapes are dry, the next stage is wiring the outer edge of the brim, followed by binding the wire. The crown is fitted and sewn to the brim and a petersham head fitting, or **sweatband**, is inserted to form the fitting.

Finally the basic hat is decorated with an appropriate **trimming**, which can change the look of the whole hat. Decoration can be kept to a minimum, but inventive milliners enjoy using silks, tulles, organzas, feathers, or flowers. The range of materials for decoration is limited only by the inventiveness of the designer. A talented milliner can be unconventional and wildly creative, bending or breaking the rules. The only criteria are the personality of the client and the occasion on which the hat is to be worn.

The fun and fascination of millinery design is that there are no fixed rules.

A classic plain style speaks with the strength of shape and form; another hat may be a fantasy creation of color, wit, and wild imagination—each has its role and purpose. Never forget though that the hat is a fashion item and that its *raison d'être* is to make a woman look stylish, sophisticated, mysterious, and beautiful.

Men are intrigued by women in hats, and women have often wished that men wore hats more often. Hats are noticed more than any other fashion item and— perhaps more important—they are almost always remembered.

The Turn of a Century

JANUARY 1, 1900: CHURCH BELLS RANG IN THE TWENTIETH CENTURY, setting off an avalanche of political, social, economic, and technical changes that would overturn many of the values and certainties of the nineteenth century. This first decade of the new century was part of the *Belle Epoque*. Meaning literally the "beautiful era," this time of fun and gaiety in France spanned the end of the nineteenth and the beginning of the twentieth century. The French capital, Paris, was the fashion center and around the world, people interested in clothes and accessories waited eagerly to find out about the latest Parisian styles.

The start of this new century was full of optimism and people looked to the future with confidence. Paris staged a World Fair and opened its first subway system to carry visitors to the Fair across the city. The Lumière brothers were showing the first moving images to enthusiastic audiences in Paris. Across the Atlantic in New York, buildings reached for the sky with the construction of the Flat Iron building, the tallest building in America.

Some things seemed to remain unchanged. After 60 years on the throne, Victoria was still Queen of Great Britain and head of a vast British empire that stretched across the world, Russia's head of state was a czar, and much of the rest of Europe was ruled by princes, kings, or emperors. Gentleman paraded around town dressed in top hats and tails, escorting ladies whose perfect hourglass figures were shaped by tight corsets and draped with voluminous, full-length skirts.

Dramatic events in the early years of the new century left no doubt that the world was changing and that life would never be quite the same again. Queen Victoria died in 1901 and in the

same year, the 25th president of the United States, William McKinley, was assassinated. In science, physicist Albert Einstein began to outline his theories on relativity and Austrian composer Gustav Mahler composed his Fifth Symphony, which evoked so well the mood and the atmosphere of these early years of the new century.

Dramatic changes in lifestyles were to affect dress and fashion throughout the twentieth century. Paris was the center of women's fashion creation, and society ladies on both sides of the Atlantic would abide to its fashion dictatorship. Men's dress had become very conservative during the nineteenth century and remained so, with the emphasis on a durable, dependable, discreet style, which was perfected by English tailors in London's Savile Row.

Men and women from all sections of society, young or old, rich or poor, had one important dress code in common. They all wore hats and they wore them all the time. There were styles appropriate for gentlemen, tradesmen, farmers, or street hawkers and to be hatless was only acceptable for beggars. Women changed their hats several times a day and would never set foot outside without a hat. Being *tête-nue* (bare-headed) was not acceptable to society.

In England, women were tired of the dark clothes that were worn during Queen Victoria's reign and welcomed a chance to wear brighter colors and enjoy a more lively lifestyle. Corsets were loosened a little, and the bustle on skirts gave way to the sensual S-line. The front of skirts shortened to show a glimpse of women's ankles, considered quite outrageous at the time.

Fantasy Hats

The ideal image for women at the time was to look fragile and delicate. A small waist was desirable, but being too thin was not, as it was a common belief at the time that very thin women had bad tempers. The new S-line was feminine and flattering, and encouraged graceful movement.

Long hair, which had been proclaimed "a woman's crowning glory" the century before, was still a great asset. It was pinned up high to accentuate a long, slim neckline.

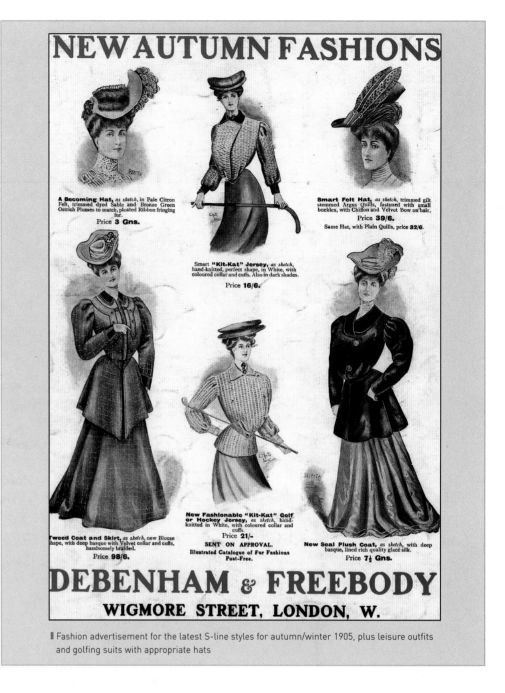

Fashion advertisement for the latest S-line styles for autumn/winter 1905, plus leisure outfits and golfing suits with appropriate hats

The hairstyles created a perfect platform for *Belle Epoque* hats which were very large and designed to balance and set off the whole female silhouette. Milliners could unleash all their creative skills and play with silks, velvets, ribbons, and artificial flowers, and most of all, feathers, lots of feathers! Plumage on hats was *le dernier cri*, the fashion that everyone had to have.

At that time in Paris there were 800 *plumassiers* or feather-making workshops, which employed about 7,000 people. Feather-makers were creative craftsmen, who prepared, dyed, and arranged all kinds of feathers mostly for milliners, but also for use in fans and home decorations. They made anything from small, spiky trimmings to colorful ostrich boas, tufts, and sprays of feathers called *aigrettes*.

There were even stuffed birds perched on hats, as if they had just swooped down from the sky. Sumptuous or delicate, feather decorations on hats swayed tantalizingly with every movement a lady made and were the perfect fashion accessory to achieve the look of dignified pride and delicate vulnerability which represented the ideal image of womanhood at the time.

Queen Alexandra

REGAL HATS OF THE DAY

The British king, Edward VII, and his beautiful wife, Queen Alexandra, were trendsetters in the new century, dictating etiquette and setting an example of taste and sophistication for upper-class circles. During her years as Princess of Wales, Alexandra received as much attention as Diana, Princess of Wales, was to have 80 years later. She was beautiful, innocent, and only 18 years old when she left Denmark for London to marry the Prince of Wales. She had been brought up in the aristocratic but relatively impoverished household of the heir to the Danish throne who had several children. Alexandra learned at an early age how to dress and look good on a budget. She even learned how to make her own hats and bonnets, which endeared her very much to her frugal mother-in-law, Queen Victoria.

Alexandra was the perfect princess, tall and slim, charming and sweet-natured. When she was crowned queen in 1902, she was 57 years old, and still looked stunning with her tiny, waspy waist. She put an end to the court mourning, which required that everybody be dressed in black for years. In complete contrast to her entourage of ladies-in-waiting, all dressed in black, she appeared wearing a dazzling, white dress.

Elegant and poised, she looked wonderful in the elaborate hat styles of the period but her free spirit was shown in stories of her borrowing her husband's hat and striding out for walks in the park wearing his **Homburg**. Having fun by breaking some of the rules did not stop her from being a dutiful wife. It was stipulated under Victorian law that a woman had "a duty to dress for her husband as well as for God." Women were regarded as decorative objects whose only aim was "to brighten up the drawing room" with their dress, manners, and appearance. Queen Alexandra perfected this art and was a fashion icon for dress designers and milliners, as well as for high society at the time.

▌Queen Alexandra and King Edward VII on board the royal yacht at Cowes in 1909. In one of the last pictures they had taken together they show themselves to be trendsetters for fashion and style. Queen Alexandra wears a *canotier* elaborately trimmed and perched high on her head, while Edward echoes the yachting scene with his sea captain's cap

Icon of the decade

▌*Belle Epoque* picture hat elaborately trimmed with ostrich plumes

Far back in history, feather decorations on hats have always been a sign of wealth and a status symbol. Plumes were available in a multitude of varieties, colors, and textures. There were shiny cockerel feathers, fluffy marabous, colorful pheasants, dramatic ostriches, wispy ospreys, herons, or bird of paradise feathers. Milliners loved using them all and the clientele of the *Belle Epoque* could not get enough of them.

A wonderful hat trimmed with beautiful bird of paradise plumes in their natural colors of emerald, spice, yellow, and cream, could cost as much as $100, which was a fortune in 1905. Feathers were imported to Europe in huge quantities from America and South Africa, as well as from all corners of the British Empire. Exotic birds all over the world suffered near extinction until the voices of conservationists started to be heard.

The RSPB (Royal Society for the Protection of Birds) was founded in 1889 in England. In the United States, the Audubon Society tried to stop the trade in wild bird feathers and raised ecological awareness among high society ladies. After repeated campaigning, Britain's Queen Alexandra agreed to ban ladies from court if they had osprey feathers on their hats. This gesture led to a ban on using the feathers of many other endangered birds. Women today still love wearing feathered hats, and milliners still love designing extravagant hats using plumes, but they have had to learn to use their ingenuity and create hats using feathers from farmed ostriches, pheasants, ducks, and cockerels.

If a hat around 1910 was not decorated with feathers, it was piled high with draped and ruched silk fabrics, nets, and veils. Velvet, satin, taffeta, and **faille** were popular materials, also available in the form of ribbons of different widths and varieties. These hat sculptures of fabrics, feathers, and ribbons had to be carefully balanced on the high and elaborate hairstyles of the day. They were also secured with long hatpins which reached a record length of 12 inches in 1910. Beautifully designed and crafted hatpins provided yet another opportunity for more creativity, this time for jewelers who produced exquisite pieces, using a wealth of metals, pearls, and semiprecious stones. Gentlemen wore top hats for formal dress

| Dinner at the theatre; a typical scene in Paris at the turn of the century, painted by Impressionist artist Jean Beraud (1849-1935)

and straw boaters for the more leisurely occasions. No man in America or Europe went outside his house or business without wearing a hat. It was a man's trademark and a gentleman's dignity and pride. Being hatless was considered impolite and socially unacceptable. Not wearing a hat also made social greetings difficult; men often took off their hats to salute passersby.

Many styles of softer and more casual hats for men came to Europe from America. The 1902 edition of the Sears, Roebuck catalogue offered as many as 65 different hat styles to choose from, without including caps. There were black silk hats for $6, men's large or full-shaped hats for $2.25, and **fedoras** for 98c. Some more unusual styles included the Governor for $2, the Railroad hat and the Roosevelt for $1. More expensive were the John B. Stetson hat (now just called a **stetson**), a Dakota style, and a Pine Ridge Scout hat for $2.50.

Suffragettes and Blue Stockings

During the first years of the new decade, ideas for the emancipation of women from across the Atlantic inspired British women to set up their own suffragette movement. Women who intellectually sympathized with

these ideas were called "blue stockings," and were regarded with great suspicion and apprehension by established society. Dress was a way of showing solidarity and their different outlook and hopes for women's lives. Rejecting the fashion ideal of the time, suffragettes pioneered Reformist clothes. They chose dresses and suits that were much simpler, practical, and seen as slightly masculine, as they broke away from the ideas of subordinated femininity.

The militant phase of the suffragette movement started in 1908. Women protested by chaining themselves to the railings of the Houses of Parliament in London demanding the right to vote. The Reform clothes influenced fashion and many other women took to wearing much simpler jackets with straighter skirts like the *trotteur* or day suit. From America came the notion of an "all day costume," and it promised to be a truly revolutionary garment which could be worn in the morning and the afternoon, reducing the need for a lady to change clothes from five times a day to only two.

Even Reform clothes were always worn with hats. They might be reduced in size and less extravagantly trimmed, but even the most militant suffragette would not campaign bareheaded. Suffragettes did not want to be seen as masculine and aggressive,

1990-2000
1980-1990
1970-1980
1960-1970
1950-1960
1940-1950
1930-1940
1920-1930
1910-1920
1900-1910

Paul Poiret

HOBBLE SKIRTS AND MAHARAJA TURBANS

Paul Poiret was 21 when the new century began. Growing up in Paris, he had soaked up the artistic atmosphere with all its forms of creativity from an early age. His career in the fashion industry started when he worked for an umbrella maker who let him have scraps of materials to take home and make into clothes for wooden dolls. Poiret also did a brief apprenticeship with the Worth brothers, English tailors who established and dominated *couture* in Paris in the second half of the nineteenth century.

Leaving Worth in 1904, Poiret opened his own business, impatient to get on with his own new ideas. Without hesitation, he set women free from restrictive, stiff corsets, replacing them with much softer girdles. He persuaded them to abandon the S-line for more comfortable, empire-line dresses, which were cut straight and left the waist unrestricted. The hobble skirt, which Poiret designed later, was an even newer idea but also restrictive because of its tightness around the ankle.

These designs were very novel ideas for the second half of the decade. Poiret's declaration in 1908, that "a dress that could not be worn in the street as well as in the drawing room was useless," was even more revolutionary, but reflected modern ideas and a vision of a world to come. Poiret's thinking was that fashion should reflect social changes and should be progressive like art.

▌Advertisement for fashionable objects of desire by Verlaine published in *Le Bon Ton*, 1920. The new styles of hats include turbans, bandeaux, and one of the first cloche shapes trimmed with *fichus* (lace handkerchiefs)

Throughout his life, he kept in close touch with the art world and commissioned the artist Paul Iribe to draw his clothes, creating very collectable illustrations which made Poiret designs famous all over the world.

In 1909, Russian ballet impressario Sergei Diaghilev brought the Ballet Russe company and theater designer Leon Bakst to Paris. The Ballet Russe inspired Poiret to design an oriental collection and to create his famous maharaja turban. This was a totally new hat style, and *avant-garde* ladies who were brave enough wore these outrageous hats to performances at the opera. Poiret was at the forefront of fashion, which supported women as they changed their role in society and embraced the changes that were to come.

In his dual role as designer and artist Poiret played an important part in the development of fashion magazines and in the art of fashion illustration. The first fashion magazine which pioneered Poiret's

illustration techniques was called the *Gazette du Bon Ton*. This arbiter of good taste published Poiret's designs until it merged with *Vogue* in 1925.

Poiret's flamboyant designs also reflected his own extravagant lifestyle. He was a big man who could never go unnoticed. His own clothes were as flamboyant as his designs, and he was never without a hat. At the extraordinary fancy-dress parties that he gave at his house, the rooms were decorated like stage sets, and Poiret always took the star part. He loved fun, food, and women, and was described by Diana Vreeland, a prominent American fashion journalist and future editor of *Vogue* magazine, as the "Sultan of Fashion."

Business-minded Poiret also started the Trunk Show, a fashion circus which traveled around Europe, his mannequins modeling the clothes, which sold in great quantities. He also went on lecture tours to America and was the first to launch a designer perfume called Rosine, named after his daughter. Celebrated by the rich and famous in Paris, London, and New York, Poiret was once invited by Margot Asquith, the wife of Britain's prime minister, to stage a fashion show at No. 10 Downing Street, the prime minister's official residence.

In later life, Poiret's inability to keep up with changes in the world of fashion led to his downfall. After the Depression in the early 1930s, the demand for expensive, exclusive garments diminished and Poiret stumbled from financial difficulties into bankruptcy. He died in 1944, in poverty, and was nearly forgotten until the young designers of the 1970s and 1980s acknowledged his contribution to twentieth-century fashion and learned to appreciate him as the great master of innovation that he truly was.

▌ Evening gown by Poiret with draped bodice, low waistline, and a skirt above the ankle, accessorized by a Maharaja turban

FASHIONABLE MILLINERY AND TWO OUTDOOR GOWNS.

as their famous leader, Sylvia Pankhurst, believed that this would not show their cause in a favorable light. In a newspaper article after a suffragette court appearance at the time, it was stressed "how feminine they looked, not big-boned or aggressive." Suffragettes favored purple, white, and green as colors that symbolize dignity, purity, fertility, and hope. It became fashionable for women to buy sashes, hat decorations, and other accessories in these colors to identify themselves with the movement and help to publicize the cause.

In Vogue

In America the first decade of the century was an era of optimism, confidence, and economic achievement. They were the golden years, when life was secure and women comfortably adapted to their roles as wives, mothers, and homemakers. These had few rights or outside interests and amused themselves with planning their wardrobe for summers in Newport or Bar Harbor, winters in Palm Beach and Bermuda, and for the regular trips to London and Paris.

The most important items were hats; no lady ever set foot outside her home without wearing one. French-influenced fashion magazines were easy reading and provided light relief from boredom with the latest temptations in fashionable millinery.

The prestigious American fashion magazine *Vogue* ran a regular supplement with reports on the latest developments in the world of millinery. Nine decades later, these excerpts from the magazine offer a fascinating picture of the fashion, society, and the designs of the time.

American Vogue, *February 1910*

Spring forecast: "A hint of the coming Mode in hats may be taken from one, worn by Miss Mary Garden at the theater…Sitting in a conspicuous place in the box chatting vivaciously with her neighbor, her large **picture hat** concealed from the public gaze her entire face and beautiful shoulders. The sweeping brim was topped by a large cheesebox crown, but it was the trimming that gave the hat the final cachet. This consisted merely of two full, heavy headed ostrich plumes in raven black which were perched jauntily at the extreme back of the crown, placed in such a way that they drooped slightly over the back…"

"Many hats will have exaggeratedly high crowns of taffeta, velvet, and tulle. Another feature will be the mingling of half a dozen bright colors which, although startling in

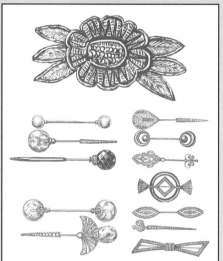

▮ **opposite far left** A salesman proves to his customer that his hats are as light as a feather by balancing them on a pair of scales

▮ **opposite near left** Fashion page from *The Sphere* magazine, illustrating refined millinery creations to accessorize the new fashion silhouette

▮ **above left** The famous Black Ascot race meeting in 1910, an event mourning the death of King Edward VII who had died on May 6, 1910, several weeks earlier

▮ **left** Fantasy hatpins helped to attach full-brimmed hats to the elaborate hair styles of the time

▮ **above** The *Vogue* "windscreen hat" designed for automobiling in 1917. The metal frame windscreen sitting on the shoulders of the wearer protected the face and could be packed away in its leather case at the end of the journey

1990–2000
1980–1990
1970–1980
1960–1970
1950–1960
1940–1950
1930–1940
1920–1930
1910–1920
1900–1910

effect, is appropriate for the year. One mode recently bought for a southern wardrobe was of a cadet blue straw model. The high, full puff-crown was of bright green taffeta and the only other trimming was a dozen cherries in the brightest shade of canary yellow."

American Vogue, *Millinery Supplement, March 1909*

"The ideal thing for wear at Palm Beach or Bermuda might be this lovely model resembling the original Persian **turban** with its size as large as permissible...Soft narrow folds of black maline tulle are finely shirred and edged with a little border of plushy, soft chenille, also in black and applied in close succession to the tulle covered foundation, swathing it completely and lending an unusual effect to the ensemble. There is a very tall, pyramid-shaped touffe of *aigrettes* decorating the front. The exquisite, delicate, fine plumage is supported by a big handsome cabochon of cut steel and stands gaily erect towering high over the top of the turban."

For an evening out, *Vogue* offers a "Coiffure for the Opera." "A narrow band of ermine wound like a Greek filet, fastened with seed pearl ornaments or a band of sable tails twisted with gold beads and fastened with a bunch of Parma violets on one side of the back."

A New Sport: Automobiling

With the arrival of the new craze for driving automobiles, milliners had to move with the times, too. They designed hats that would allow women to climb into cars and drive along bumpy roads and dirt tracks at speed. The motorcar would later be blamed for the demise of hat wearing and millinery, but in those early days ladies would not be without a hat, not even in a car. Motoring veils were invented looking like beekeepers' nets, they shrouded the whole head in muslin or silk chiffon. Some veils had lace panels set into the front so that the wearer could take a peek at the oncoming dangers or obstacles ahead.

The year 1910 drew the final curtain over the *Belle Epoque*. In Britain, King Edward VII died a few weeks before the summer racing season. Rather than canceling the races all together, Edwardian society decided to show their mourning by staging the famous "Black Ascot" when everybody arrived dressed in black from head to toe. All the milliners had to work overtime producing hundreds of black hats and "Black Ascot" has gone down as a memorable event in the history of the Ascot race meeting.

The Bonnet

STYLES OF MASTERS AND SERVANTS

A frilly lace *boudoir* bonnet worn by American actress Billie Burke in the operetta *The Duchess of Dantzic*

The **bonnet** is probably the oldest hat style in history. Leather bonnets were worn by noblemen at the time of William the Conqueror in eleventh-century England, and remained the headgear of the nobility during the Middle Ages when they were made from embroidered velvet and brocades. "Bonnet" was curiously the collective name for all kinds of men's hats until women's fashion took it over and developed endless variations and styles, but all bonnets covered the ears and could be tied or fastened under the chin.

The 1700s *fontange* bonnet was a frilly headdress supported on a wire frame called a *commode* and was attached to a cap. Bows and ribbons called knots were tied under the chin to hold this high construction on the head.

A few years later the mob cap was designed for "undress" occasions. A lace border framed the face and had lappets hanging down, known as kissing strings. Towards the end of the eighteenth century ladies graced themselves by wearing the *voluptueuse*, which was a *coiffure de nuit*, designed to protect the horsehair-stuffed wigs, and looked charming decorated with ribbons, beads, and tassels.

The capote bonnet had a stiffened brim, which blinkered the view. In the Charente area of southwestern France, the *quichenotte* (or *kichenotte*) derived from "kiss me not," which the pretty French maidens whispered to fend off the English soldiers during the religious wars.

The poke-bonnet followed and resembled more the shape of a proper hat with a high crown and deep brim which often had a frilled edge.

It was as always demurely fastened under the chin, but this time without a bow. The *bibi* bonnet (or lampshade bonnet) had a kind of short pleated curtain which hung at the back of the neck, called *bavolet*.

The nineteenth century was the hey-day of the bonnet. The angle of the brim and crown varied, and they became more and more elaborately decorated, framing the face and always demurely fastened under the chin. There were deep halos obscuring the face and smaller ones set further back to show a curled fringe. Alexandra, the future Princess of Wales arrived in England in 1863 wearing a white bonnet decorated with roses.

Toward the end of the nineteenth century, Charles Frederick Worth designed very small bonnets for Empress Eugenie in Paris. She wanted her face to be seen, so bonnets ended up as little hats perched on the head and held with a soft bow under the chin. Eventually, hats took over completely and bonnets were relegated to the servants' quarters where different styles were dictated by the hierarchy of life "downstairs." Girls in service wore caps suited to their rank and the most important parlor maids wore different headgear in the morning and the afternoon.

The 1920s brought a fashion for the *boudoir* cap, a lingerie hat worn with costly silk negligées. Wallis Simpson, the future Duchess of Windsor, was photographed wearing a bonnet on a 1936 cruise. This might have been a practical thought, but it aroused negative comments on the society pages, describing the future Duchess as being as ridiculous as an "adult in a baby's hat." Grace Kelly looked beautiful in her bridal bonnet designed by the famous milliner Rudolph, for her wedding to Monaco's Prince Rainier.

Over the decades bonnets went out of fashion, until the Sixties brought back glimmers of the past with fur bonnets in mink and Persian lamb, as well as designs in soft velour felts and jerseys. The tradition of Easter bonnets, which had arrived from America, flourished in England for many years. Milliners used to make quite outrageous straw hats and decorate them in the spirit of spring with ribbons and flowers. Prizes were given to the most flamboyant designs, and the winners were usually photographed by the local newspaper.

Today the only bonnet-wearers left are the women of the Salvation Army as part of their reassuringly traditional uniforms. At the end of the twentieth century, they are the only relics of this historical style—as even babies have switched to baseball caps. But fashion traditionally has a habit of making unexpected U-turns and bonnets might be reinvented and become a fashion craze again. Who knows?

▌ *above* French impressionist painter Auguste Renoir (1941-1919) adored painting women in hats. *Danse à la Campagne*, painted in 1883, portrays a seductive young lady wearing a red bonnet perched at the back of her head

▌ *right* Three nineteenth-century bonnets, displayed in the Musée du Chapeau, Chazelles, France. From left to right: a *bibi* bonnet in lace and tulle with a satin bow, dated 1885; a small round cap in black tulle embroidered with gold thread, dated 1870; a mourning bonnet in black crepe, 1890

Titanic Changes

THE SINKING OF THE "UNSINKABLE" *TITANIC* ON ITS MAIDEN VOYAGE from Europe to the United States in 1912 shocked people around the world. The luxury liner, which was such a symbol of the glamor and confidence of its time, collided with an iceberg and sank to the bottom of the sea. Only a handful of the 1,513 passengers were saved from the icy Atlantic waters. The chill felt after the *Titanic* went down seemed like a portent of the momentous events to come.

In August, 1914, Germany declared war on Russia and France and Britain's bid for neutrality was rejected, forcing them to mobilize their forces against Wilhelm II. The German Kaiser also happened to be Queen Victoria's grandson and a cousin to the British King. Many people thought that this dispute would be settled by Christmas, but it escalated into the Great War with all its horror and terrible consequences. The United States remained neutral until 1917, when its ships were attacked by German U-boats in the Atlantic. Later the same year, the Russian Revolution followed. By 1918, the Austro-Hungarian Empire had been dismantled. Like a house of cards, many European royal courts, and with them their social values, collapsed. The wind of change was suddenly blowing from a different direction.

Lifestyles and fashion were affected dramatically. In the prewar years, some women had kept their elaborate S-line dresses and their rigid corsets, but many others embraced the influence of French designer Paul Poiret in fashion and changed to looser clothes, some even daring to wear harem pants for the first time. Fashion was getting more comfortable, but was still restrictive. The hobble skirt was tight around the ankles and made women walk with tiny, shuffling steps, like puppets on a string. Society

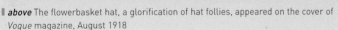

❚ *above* The flowerbasket hat, a glorification of hat follies, appeared on the cover of *Vogue* magazine, August 1918

❚ *above* *Vogue* cover February 1917 by Helen Dryden, who liked to capture the image of ladies of culture with simple hat styles

ladies accepted the dictates of fashion and even embarked on the craze for tango dancing, which had arrived from South America. They must have had fun hobbling away in their tango shoes, showing dainty ankles wrapped in criss-cross ribbons. Hats were, of course, still worn at all times, even for dancing.

Men appeared about town wearing dark suits and Homburg hats, a fashion which the late British King, Edward VII, had launched after a visit to Homburg in Germany. Men's hats had diversified into several different shapes before the war and not everyone wore tall black top hats anymore. Sensing the mood for less height, hatmakers produced shallower versions of the topper, which were also available in gray.

The **bowler** hat had also been invented and was considered a younger man's hat. Another model, the **cheerer**, was like a bowler but had a flat top and was preferred by farmers and country folk. For leisurely summer pursuits, the straw **boater** was favorite. In Britain, **deerstalkers**, familiar now to many only from Sherlock Holmes stories, were the hats for sports and hunting. The soft **trilby**, named after a well-known Victorian novel by George du Maurier, was favored as an image of intellectual Bohemianism, which was the *avant-garde* thinking at the time. Bohemian men and women wore tunics and smocks and wrapped short or long capes around themselves instead of formal coats.

Hats for women lost their large brims and grew in height instead, which complemented the new fluid silhouettes much better. Narrower brims with substantial crowns and high brimless **toques** (derived from the Italian *tocca*) were fashionable and fitted beautifully on the shorter, but still voluminous hairstyles. Favored materials were silk fabrics, like velvet, satin, taffeta, and *moiré*, which could be draped, ruched, or shirred, to form a rich background for trimmings of artificial flowers and feathers. Altogether the look was solid, serious, and quite heavy.

The image of Britain's Queen Mary, wife of the new king, George V, epitomizes the rich but sober style of hats before the war. Ladies

Mary Pickford

POOR LITTLE RICH GIRL

Mary Pickford was everybody's favorite golden girl. Her films provided escape from the harsh realities of life for millions of ordinary people whose own lives were very gloomy during these traumatic years. While she epitomized the image of a sweet little girl on screen, in reality she was a very determined and clever actress, becoming a multi-millionairess at the age of 27. She married her Prince Charming, actor Douglas Fairbanks, and their home, Pickfair, became Hollywood's dream palace of the 1920s. This golden couple set fashion trends and both looked great in hats. Mary was demure and charming in pastel-colored straw hats, with blonde corkscrew curls framing her face, or more mature *toques* and cloches. Douglas Fairbanks, meanwhile, looked dashing in a debonair straw boater.

Douglas and Mary Fairbanks, the golden couple of the Twenties, say farewell to Charlie Chaplin on their departure to England

Icon of the decade

junknown © Vogue/Condé Nast Publications Ltd

 A charming bandeau hat by Lanvin from the 1918-19 collection

A high draped toque by Lewis accessorized the new slim silhouette and appeared in *Vogue* magazine, December 1917

still needed a diverse millinery wardrobe, because etiquette required that they change their hats at different times of the day. Evening hats were fashionable for dinner functions and going to the opera. Inventive milliners designed elaborate **bandeau** called *chapeaux niniches* (literally "little nothings") and decorated them with pearls, ribbons, feathers, and flowers. This was the last flourish of evening hats for a while. They did not reappear until 1919, when the Parisian authorities lifted the ban on evening dress which had been imposed during the war years.

Women at War

The war put an end to the theatrical look in fashion and women had to think about practical clothes. Women who joined different war groups had to wear uniforms. These styles of uniforms were not discussed in the fashion pages of *Vogue*, but they had a great influence on fashion thinking and also prompted a great boost in women's self-confidence. Women might be working in factories or join the Women's Land Army but also took on jobs as refuse collectors, streetcar drivers, lamplighters, or chimney sweeps. Each job had its uniform, with a hat showing rank and position.

Uniforms were sometimes embellished with a little scarf or jewelry, adding a touch of femininity to this more masculine style of dress. Some women joined the soldiers in the battle zones and worked as helpers behind the lines, often wearing the proudest uniform of all, that of a Red Cross nurse.

Women in Sport

Women in 1915 were leaner, slimmer, and fitter and not afraid of new sporting activities which required a set of fashionable clothing. In this new era, women were bicycling, mountain climbing, bathing, ice-skating, and they had also taken up playing golf and tennis. American dancer Isadora Duncan made headlines with her uninhibited movement and wild gypsy dancing which was her expression of freedom in mind and spirit. Milliners were quick to devise new forms of appropriate headgear to accessorize all the new sporting activities and created bathing headdresses from rubberized satin, brimmed straw sports **panamas**, draped bandeaux for tennis, soft **berets** for golfing, and furry **Cossack** hats for winter sports.

Lady Diana Cooper

MILLINERY MANNERS

Lady Diana Manners, later to become Lady Diana Cooper, was one of the outstanding beauties of this century. Admirers were magnetically drawn to her, and she was written about in British society magazines and the fashion press throughout her life. Youngest daughter of England's Duke of Rutland, Diana had had a passion for dressing up with her sisters and friends from a very early age. She followed her unconventional mother, who had also rejected the demure Edwardian styles, and she expressed her free spirit by wearing an "odd and artistic type of dress," as reported by American *Vogue* in 1910.

Part of a circle of high-spirited young women who liked to be known as the *Corrupt Coterie*, Diana and her friends were bored with conventional fashion and liked to shock with the boldness of their dress and style. Diana made headlines on her first visit to Venice, Italy, by dressing in a white naval officer's cloak and large hat with a plume of cockerel feathers. She dressed a little more conventionally after she married Duff Cooper in 1919, but never lost her taste for theatrical eccentricity. Cecil Beaton, photographer, *Vogue* fashion writer, and aesthete, remembers her appearing "in a scarlet **tricorn** hat and red cape" at a hunt ball in Chantilly, France, in 1949. She was reportedly seen wearing coral pink at a party in 1982 when she was well over 80 years old.

Lady Diana Cooper was one of those much-applauded leaders of fashion whom milliners and designers love to dress. Like many of her successors during the century, Diana Cooper was a star and role model representing hope and excitement for many ordinary women, brightening up their lives during the gloomy days of World War I.

❚ Lady Diana Cooper disembarks from HMS Homeric on her arrival in England from New York on October 18, 1924. A lady of exquisite style and fine dress sense, she wears a felt bicorn trimmed with coquades, pulled down deep over her forehead

Wartime Britain and a uniformed bus conductress at work on a double-decker bus in snowy London. Uniform hats were obligatory and their different styles have had an enduring influence on fashion

Elegant bathing suits and hats designed by Jean Patou, Paris 1926

The First Cloches

To the great regret of milliners, fashion never returned to the prewar ornate styles. Hat designs had to adapt themselves to suit the newly emerging lifestyles of a changed world. After the war, the beauty in hats lay in the simplicity of design. As early as 1917, French milliner Lucy Hamar had designed the first **cloche** hats, which were heralded by *Vogue* as "the newest hats from Paris."

The early versions worn by socialites like England's Lady Diana Cooper or the Parisian Duchesse de Gramont, did not look at all like the bell-shaped hat which was to became the craze in the 1920s. The early cloche hats had flexible, wide brims and square crowns. They were mostly black and decorated only with very discreet, contrasting trimmings, or even simpler with just a single piece of jewelry. The brim could be pinned up in the front or at the back, and the hat could be shaded with dotted veiling, adding an air of elegant sophistication and style.

New York, the Center of American Fashion

The Great War had also brought significant changes to the American fashion industry, which up until then had been completely dependent on Paris. Between 1914 and 1918 little exchange was possible, as shipping across the Atlantic was impossible. Fashion businesses in New York tried out the designs of talented, young American designers, rather than waiting to copy Parisian originals. A competition in 1916 invited dress and hat designs, which were produced and publicized as "American-made Bonwit Teller Creations." This prompted the *Ladies Home Journal* to be the first magazine to start writing articles about American fashion innovations, putting New York designers well and truly on the map. A small example of American fashion exports to Europe was recorded when a young lady, dressed in a chic outfit designed and made in New York walked the streets of Paris and launched the fashion of *le walking suit* in France. New York was definitely the capital of American fashion and style watchers would take a close interest to see which trend was accepted or rejected by Manhattan.

▌Military-inspired khaki suit with soldiers' beret, designed by Max Meyer, New York, for his ready-to-wear range in the years of World War I

▌The first cloche hat by Lucie Hamar, appearing in *Vogue*, February 1917, with a wide brim, deep flat crown, and wisps of fantasy trimming

Particularly American is the tendency, apparent in this mid-1910s ready-to-wear skating costume by Max Meyer, to design clothes for fairly vigorous activities in an intentionally feminine idiom. European sports clothes for ladies were usually translated literally from those worn by men. The Library, Fashion Institute of Technology, New York

▌A mid-1910s skating costume by Max Meyer, New York, who was renowned for his feminine outfits designed for sporting activities

▌A charming winter turban with high topknot pulled down deep over the new short hair styles of the 1920s

1990–2000

1980–1990

1970–1980

1960–1970

1950–1960

1940–1950

1930–1940

1920–1930

1910–1920

1900–1910

Gabrielle Chanel

CLASSICAL SIMPLICITY

Gabrielle Chanel, known better as Coco, found fame and fortune by changing the look of women's fashion in the twentieth century, and could be described as the most influential designer of the century. She had a vision of style for women and turned this into a successful business, creating *haute couture* clothes, accessories, and her inimitable perfume, Chanel No 5, which made her name recognized throughout the world.

Chanel's early life at the turn of the century had humble beginnings. Having lost her mother as a child, she was brought up in a convent where she learned to sew. The mother superior of the convent recommended her to a dressmaker in town and *la petite Coco* soon learned to support herself with her sewing skills, as well as by singing at the local café concerts at night.

This led Coco into the world of the *demimondaines*, an unconventional social circle, which was not always considered entirely respectable. She met Etienne Balsan, who was to be her first lover and benefactor. He was rich, had a passion for horses, and lived surrounded by friends and courtesans on an estate in La Croix-Saint-Ouen, near Paris. Coco moved into his circle of friends, but always stood out by wearing very simple, modest, homemade outfits which contrasted with the showy style preferred by the other women. She liked to be regarded as special and eccentric. Stylishly dressed in riding outfits made by a man's tailor, she showed off her horseriding skills, which also endeared her to Balsan.

In 1908, she persuaded Balsan to let her set up her first business at his apartment in the Boulevard des Malesherbes, in Paris. It was to be a select *Salon de Chapeaux*, frequented by actresses, singers, and friends of the *demimonde*. Coco was adept with her hands and made much-admired hats for Emilienne d'Alençon, a celebrated actress and also a friend of Balsan's. She would also buy basic straw boaters from the Galeries Lafayette department store and alter and trim them for her friends. Her millinery creations were modern, neat, unfussy hats with the classic flair and charm that were to become the hallmarks of the Chanel style of *haute couture*.

© Chanel—drawing by Karl Lagerfeld

Design sketches by Karl Lagerfeld, 1991, in which he follows in the spirit of simple elegance created by Coco Chanel

As the hat business expanded, Coco moved into her own premises in the Rue Cambon. In 1910, she opened Chanel Mode, making her name as a milliner. She was helped by the second man in her life, Arthur "Boy" Chapel, a rich English businessman who was also an excellent polo player. Her relationship with Boy Chapel was a great influence on her life and opened doors into illustrious international society. They were often seen at the opera, or dining at Maxim's. Her hats were celebrated and worn by well-known actresses of the day, as well as being modeled by Coco herself for fashion magazines.

Her reputation spread far and wide, and Chanel was asked to design hats for Gabrielle Dorziat who was to play the leading role in a new play by writer Guy de Maupassant at the Théâtre de Vaudeville. The clothes were designed by an established *couturier*, Doucet, and the hats by young Gabrielle Chanel. This brought even more publicity and a new clientele which was seeking the fresh, modern look of Chanel's designs. By 1913, Chanel Mode was financially independent and generating a profit.

The summer of 1913 brought the breakthrough into dress design. Chanel took a shop in the elegant seaside resort of Deauville, on the Normandy coast, where *le tout Paris* (the whole of Paris) was to be seen promenading along the seafront. Strategically placed between the casino and the exclusive Normandy Hotel, the Chanel shop attracted the attention of Baroness de Rothschild and other ladies who abandoned their allegiance to Poiret in favor of Coco Chanel.

▌The "*garçonne* look" was the new youthful fashion of straight, uncorseted clothes, giving women physical freedom they had not enjoyed for centuries

As her fame spread, the *haute couture* house in the Rue Cambon in Paris grew into an international business. Chanel dressed high society and Hollywood stars. In 1931, she was offered a million dollars to leave Paris and go to Hollywood and design for the MGM studio. She dressed actress Gloria Swanson for the film *Tonight or Never*, but friction between the two headstrong ladies of film and fashion led to Coco's departure after only a year.

Coco Chanel's style weathered all the fashion changes over the decades and survived the closure of the salon during World War II. The classic, timeless Chanel suit was developed in 1954 and remains Coco's epitaph after her death in 1971. It is still reinvented for every collection by new designer Karl Lagerfeld, who has given the Chanel label its modernity without losing the style of its famous creator.

The Topper

A TALL HAT FOR GENTLEMEN AIMING HIGH

Rigid, black, shiny, and tall, the top hat, or **topper**, epitomized Victorian Britain and its values, which, just like the hat, made a great impact on the whole world. Until well into the twentieth century, the formal day wear for men of black frock or tail coat, black trousers, and a stiff collared shirt, was not complete without a top hat. The shiny **silk beaver** hat was originally a French invention and became the status symbol for the nineteenth-century gentleman, replacing the cocked tricorns and **bicorns** fashionable in the previous century. With its narrow brim, it performed its task as an excellent riding hat which did not blow off easily. A refined French version became the conventional headgear for gentlemen in Europe, Britain, and America.

Lords, politicians, ministers, doctors, even judges out of court wore top hats when walking about town or lounging in their clubs. A symbol of wealth, dignity, and social standing, the top hat was high and regal and made men look taller, more imposing, and handsome.

Men-about-town like English Regency dandies and their French counterparts wore toppers with panache and flair and the hat became a symbol of *bon vivre* (high living). Count Danilo, the much-loved playboy figure from Franz Lehar's operetta *The Merry Widow*, is unforgettable in his silk hat, stumbling drunkenly out of the prestigious restaurant Maxim's in fashionable Paris. He waves his hat about with exuberant charm, dances, sings, and greets passing ladies, then uses his hat to cover his face while he dozes. He could not be Count Danilo without his top hat!

The arrival of the top hat in England from Paris, in the late 1790s, was greeted with outrage and mockery. Hatter John Hetherington had made a shiny, black silk plush hat in a new, high chimney-pot style. As he walked down Whitehall proudly wearing it for the first time, the hat caused quite a commotion. The *St. James's Gazette* reported that the hat was "calculated to frighten timid people." According to various historical accounts, Mr Hetherington's walk caused outrage and an angry riot among Londoners, who pelted the poor man with whatever they could find on the road. As horses and carts provided the transportation of the day, it was a messy business, but the hat passed its test with flying colors. It stayed firmly on Mr Hetherington's head, protecting its master from injury. Strange to think that this revolutionary headgear would became a symbol of authority and conservative values in the nineteenth century.

The top hat was not really made from black silk, but from beaver felt, which was brushed and highly polished after being treated with mercury nitrate, a chemical mixture later proven to cause "Mad Hatter's disease." A physical disorder which affected the nervous system, this condition was caused by inhaling toxic fumes used for felting animal hair. The symptoms were also recognized in the United States where Mad Hatter's disease was called the Danbury Shakes after the town in Connecticut, the center of top hat manufacture in America.

▌ Henri Raymonde de Toulouse-Lautrec's (1864-1901) portrait of Monsieur Louis Pascal, a typical turn-of-the-century gentleman who was rarely seen without his top hat

At James Lock & Co., Ltd, the traditional hatmakers in London, people still ask for fine silk plush hats, but they are no longer made. The only chance of acquiring one is by having a top hat in the family, or finding one in an antique shop. Locks have a restoration service but have great difficulties with younger men's head sizes, which have grown since their grandfathers' days.

Today, elegant gray toppers appear at summer weddings all over the world. The most high-profile outing for toppers in England is at the Royal Ascot race meeting, the high point of the summer horseracing season. Even in the modern hatless world, men who are invited into the Royal Enclosure at Ascot or who are accompanying a lady there, are obliged to wear a black or gray topper.

Most practical, late twentieth-century men hire their hats for the day. Years ago, Lock & Co. would store customers' hats swathed in tissue-packed boxes. Like Sleeping Beauty, the hats waited for early June, when they would be taken out, brushed, and polished for one glorious day at Royal Ascot, then put back again into the dark boxes to wait for another year.

At the turn of the century, when the topper had been established for well over one hundred years, articles began circulating in London newspapers suggesting that "the snobbery of wearing a top hat" was outdated. They even demanded that the Prince of Wales, the future King Edward VII, should take a lead and stop wearing the hat. New ideas of democracy and equality did not go well with one man being above another, even if this was only because he wore a taller hat.

In Paris, where the French Revolution of 1789 had settled France's notions about democracy a hundred years earlier, *Belle Epoque* men-about-town enjoyed themselves without a second thought. They preferred a *chapeau claque*, a collapsible version of the top hat that made a sharp noise when it was struck against the thigh to operate the springs that made the crown jump up. This ingenious invention by Monsieur Gibus, also known as the "opera," made storage very much easier. The wearer could also hold the hat flat under his arm, giving it the other name of *chapeau bras* (arm hat).

The top hat also became identified with magicians and conjurers. The crown is roomy enough to hide rabbits, pigeons, or handkerchiefs that magicians pull from their hats. The topper also imparts an air of authority, elegance, and mysticism to the magician, delighting both children and adults.

Occasionally, the topper has assumed an erotic aura when worn by women reversing male-female roles. Marlene Dietrich, appearing as Amy Jolly in the 1933 film *Morocco*, was dressed in a black tail suit, a top hat pushed jauntily to the back of her head, and smoking a cigarette, looking extremely provocative and sexy. Fred Astaire made the topper a "dancing hat" and paints an unforgettable picture gliding along the dancefloor in black top hat and tails.

Contemporary hat designer Philip Treacy was inspired by the topper when creating a hat for the 1993 wedding of Serena Stanhope and Viscount Linley, the son of Princess Margaret. The young, blond Viscountess appeared in her going-away outfit wearing a silver sequinned Treacy hat and the press had a field day. The reinvented topper had stolen the show!

London designer Stephen Jones designed a series of "miniature toppers" in the 1990s, becoming his trademark look on the catwalk and in many fashion magazines. This prompted a wave of demand for women's toppers in the millinery sections of the major London stores. Worn with elegant jackets and trousers, the hats looked stylish and glamorous. Power dressing had finally helped women to take another male bastion, the traditional top hat.

top Gentlemen about town, the "Bond Street Loungers," all faithful customers of Lock's of St. James, the traditional gentlemen's hatters

above Royal Ascot race meeting, held at the Queen's own race course, is the highlight of the English summer season. The dress code for men invited into the Royal Enclosure is black or gray morning suit and top hat

Crazy about Hats

THE TWENTIES WAS A CRAZY, FUN DECADE, WHEN THE WORLD WAS relatively peaceful and everyone who had lived through the horrors of the Great War was happy to be alive. The storm of the war years had past, and the vow was that there would never be another war. People were full of drive and optimism for the future; receptive to fresh ideas and a new outlook on life.

The exuberance, inventiveness, and productivity on both sides of the Atlantic brought a general prosperity which was expressed in lifestyles, art, and fashion. Men and many single women worked and had disposable income to spend on the variety of goods produced by thriving businesses and factories. Electricity had arrived in many homes, many households tuned in to wireless radios, some even had a telephone. In America, machines to wash clothes had been invented and splendid automobiles were available for people who could afford them. American aviator Charles Lindbergh made the first solo non-stop flight across the Atlantic, and the first commercial airline services between Europe and America were operating. New music called jazz became popular, and wild modern dances like the tango and the Charleston formed the entertainment. Women's continuing struggle for civil rights began to bear fruit and in the United States women gained the right to vote in 1920.

Women's clothing changed as radically as their lives. Clothes were loose and straight, liberating the body from stiff-boned corsets. Skirt lengths were above the ankle and getting shorter all the time, reaching knee length by 1927. The feminine ideal was the *garçonne* look, named after the heroine of a controversial novel of the same name by French writer Victor Margueritte, published in 1922. The *garçonne* look demanded a boyish, slim body, short hair

Smart and ornate Twenties dresses and coats accessorized with ropes of fake pearls and indispensable little cloche hats

Caroline Reboux, the *grande modiste Parisienne*, designed this charming straw cloche trimmed with cockerel feathers and roses. This illustration first appeared in *Vogue*, March 1922

cut in a bob, seductive make-up, and a practical, emancipated style of clothing.

The concept of a liberated, self-confident young woman was shocking to the

Gloria Swanson was the icon of the decade

wearing her hair short, she enjoyed outdoor activities and based her designs on her own lively lifestyle. Chic and classic simplicity in dress was Chanel's hallmark, including easy-to-wear jackets, skirts, and blouses, small elegant hats, and other fashion accessories. A more democratic way of dressing that was accessible to more women and not just to the exclusive few in high society was born.

Gloria Swanson

THE GLITTERING STAR OF THE TWENTIES

Legendary 1920s *femme fatale*, Gloria Swanson ranks high among Hollywood stars. In the movies and her private life, she embodied the frivolity and folly of the decade. An all-American girl from Chicago with an explosive mixture of European ancestry, Swanson was starstruck from the first time she stood in front of a camera in 1915. She went to Hollywood and became a silent movie queen, before reviving her career in the talkies of the 1930s.

One of Swanson's most famous films was *Madame Sans-Gène*, directed by Léonce Perret. Set at the beginning of the nineteenth century it tells the story of a French laundry girl who marries a *maréchal* (brigadier-general) in the French army. She meets the Emperor of France, Napoleon, and tells him that he owes her money from the days when she did his laundry. After shooting the film in France, Gloria Swanson returned to a tumultuous welcome in New York on the arm of her new husband, the Marquis de la Falaise, a real-life French aristocrat. French and American flags flew all over Times Square and the couple was greeted like royalty.

Gloria Swanson was known for employing liveried footmen in powdered wigs and satin kneebreeches at her Hollywood home. A lover of silk gowns, satin lingerie, exquisite fur coats, and glittering headdresses, she looked devastatingly sexy in turbans and chiffon scarves. As a fashion icon, she was often described as a "clotheshorse" by critics. Petite, with a typical flat-chested 1920s figure, she had huge, crystal-clear eyes, fine brows, and cupid-bow lips.

Gloria Swanson could transmit a full range of emotions and, as a superstar on and off screen, she personified the glamor and madness of the 1920s. Her tiny, slim figure and her energy made her the most glamorous woman to dress *pour le sport* (sports fashion), a term Jean Patou had created in the twenties.

A special tribute to Swanson made in 1967 could have been her epitaph: "Long before Hollywood made stars, there were stars who made Hollywood."

right Gloria Swanson (1897-1983) in her star role of *Madame Sans-Gène*, looking ice cool in a demure lampshade bonnet, edged in silk and trimmed with feathers

AUGUST
Metropolitan

Midsummer
Fiction
Number

20¢

Draped turban cloche hat of the late Twenties, perfect for young "flappers" and their fast and reckless lifestyles

▌ *Vogue* magazine cover March 1927, depicting a blue cloche with diamanté hatpin. Nighttime New York skyscrapers provide the glamorous backdrop

▌ Soft crocheted cap for evening wear created by Jeanne Lanvin

1990–2000

1980–1990

1970–1980

1960–1970

1950–1960

1940–1950

1930–1940

1920–1930

1910–1920

1900–1910

In addition to Coco Chanel, the most influential *haute couture* designer in the 1920s was Madeleine Vionnet, who earned a place in fashion history for inventing the bias-cut. With a perfect understanding of fabrics and cut, she often designed dresses by simply draping a length of fabric around her client and pinning and cutting it on the body.

Caroline Reboux was Madeleine Vionnet's counterpart in hat design. The first in a long line of Parisian *grandes modistes* (milliners) to gain international recognition, she is still remembered decades after her death. Her favorite materials were clean, structured ones like felt. She sometimes adopted methods similar to Madeleine Vionnet, creating hats by cutting and folding

the fabrics directly on a customer's head. A doyenne of simplicity, she avoided adding excessive decoration and preferred simple motifs which complemented the line and style of the hat.

A pupil of Caroline Reboux, Madame Agnès became equally famous, her fame reaching across the Atlantic. She established her own salon in the Rue du Faubourg St-Honoré in 1917 and remained in the forefront of fashion throughout her career, adapting her hat designs to trends in fashion as well as art. Her witty and original touches in millinery were well known. Like Italian-born designer Elsa Schiaparelli, Madame Agnès found her ultimate inspiration in the surrealistic trends of the 1930s.

The *haute couture* houses of Molyneux and Lanvin were known for their elegant designs, which were much loved by aristocrats and high society in Paris, New York, and London. Both designers had in-house millinery workshops and their hat designers' creations were sold under the name of the *haute couture* house. Clients enjoyed a complete service and could choose outfits alongside a hat, both created on the premises, that strongly reflected the style of the design house.

Hats changed beyond all recognition from large and complicated works of art that had to be carefully placed on the head and held on with a hatpin to small-brimmed pull-on cloche hats, perfect for carefree walks

Jean Patou

HISPANO SUIZAS, SUNTANS, AND GREEN HATS

Jean Patou was a Parisian designer whose ideas about dress were a perfect reflection of the spirit of the Twenties. His neat, sleek *couture* style fitted the new image of the emancipated and modern society woman. Society women toured in luxury Hispano Suiza cars, played tennis or golf at Deauville on the French Atlantic coast, holidayed in Biarritz, southwest France, skied in St Moritz, Switzerland, or simply met up with friends in Parisian cafés wearing a chic cloche hat.

According to Jean Patou's biographer, Meredith Etherington-Smith, the designer was "a modernist with a strong sense of tradition." Patou clothes were perfectly cut and had an uncluttered look, making the flamboyant and theatrical clothes of the previous decade look dated. His greatest gift to twentieth-century women was his design ideas encapsulated in the catchphrase *pour le sport* meaning literally "for sport," reflecting a young, new look that became a Twenties craze.

Jean Patou himself seemed tailor-made for the 1920s. Standing over six foot tall, he was slim, well-groomed, and elegant with dark, glossy hair and bright eyes. The son of a well-to-do family from Normandy in northern France, he remained close to his roots all his life. As a man of courage and grace, he did not hesitate to join up for the Great War in 1914. He had only just opened a new *haute couture* salon under his own name in the Rue St-Florentin in Paris and had to leave his collection and business in the hands of his family, especially his sister Madeleine, who was his inspiration, model, and steadfast support throughout his life. After four years of war, he returned in 1919 with a different outlook on life. He had a better understanding of ordinary working people which made him a kind and understanding *patron* (boss) who was remembered with affection by his workforce long after his untimely death in 1936.

Jean Patou's clothes *pour le sport*, his heritage to twentieth-century women, which modernized the established concept of fashion

The following few years were an uphill struggle and were full of financial difficulties. It was hard to foresee that by the mid-Twenties, the Maison Patou would be a recognized *haute couture* house with business interests in the United States and a select private clientele, including some of the most famous movie stars of the time.

Like Chanel, Patou recognized the importance of accessories in his salon. He established a millinery *atelier* on the top floor of his *couture* house, which remained an important part of the business until the 1970s. The most lucrative accessory in his fashion empire was the collection of perfumes. First was *Amour-Amour*, followed by *Sais-je*, and *Adieu Sagesse*, but the

Wearing Patou's draped headband, Suzanne Lenglen of France is on court with her ladies' doubles partner, Bunny Ryan of the USA, at the Wimbledon Lawn Tennis Championship of 1924. Described as "hideously chic," it started a new fashion in millinery

best known is *Joy*, a classic among perfumes and still marketed today as the costliest scent in the world.

French tennis champion Suzanne Lenglen made headlines when she appeared at Wimbledon in 1921 wearing a pleated skirt, sleeveless cardigan, and a bright orange headband. This chic, casual outfit transformed her instantly from an excellent tennis champion into a fashion icon, admired by women spectators on Centre Court. Suzanne Lenglen had been dressed entirely by Patou and he could not have wished for a better model. Draped headbands became the latest craze, and not just for tennis players. Lenglen continued to be dressed by Patou and became the first sports star to wear and promote designer clothing.

The Patou workshop in the Rue St-Florentin was busy making hats *pour le sport* for women to look sporty and chic. Apart from the tennis bandeau, there were small turned-up brims for golf, shallow cloche hats for riding, and fur hats for skiing. Most famous of all were the many variations of the *Green Hat*, a green felt cloche made famous by the best-selling novel by Michael Arlen of the same name. Iris Storm, the heroine of the book, could have come straight from the pages of Patou's sketchbook: "...tall, not very tall, but as tall as becomes a woman. Her hair in the shadow of her hat, may have been any color, but I dared swear that there was a tawny whisper to it." The story found further fame when it was immortalized in the film *A Woman of Affairs*, with Hollywood stars Greta Garbo, Douglas Fairbanks Jr., and John Gilbert.

It was not the first time in fashion history that a novelist had used a hat to help paint a picture and a mood, nor was it the first time that the hat had stolen the show.

An impeccable Patou riding outfit with whipcord breeches, shirt and tie in *tussore* silk and a well-fitting gray-beige riding hat. This illustration appeared in *Harper's Bazaar*, 1925

around town. The bell-shaped cloche looked fun and sophisticated, and pulled right down to eye level, which gave it a soft femininity and mysterious sexiness. These new hats went down in fashion history and are recognized worldwide as the 1920s cloche.

For the first time in history, this change in hat fashion was consumer-led and milliners had to follow their clients' wishes. The established *grandes modistes*, upmarket Parisian milliners, wanted to stop the craze for little cloche hats, considering it bad for business. *Modiste* Caroline Reboux protested against the cloche, claiming that it would be the end of millinery, something which has, of course, been predicted so many times since. Even Lucie Hamar, the inventor of the cloche, joined the Parisian milliners in a chorus of disapproval, as they feared that the sheer uniformity of the hat would result in them losing business.

All the protests were in vain, because the closefitting style of the cloche had become universally popular and suited women's new lifestyles. From aristocratic duchesses to shopworkers—known as *midinettes* in Paris—all women loved wearing such a practical, flirtatious, and sexy hat.

Responding to the simple lines of the cloche's basic bell shape, millinery salons in Paris showed their creativity with trimmings and decorations of infinite variety. Cloche hats were made from felt, straw, or fabric, and could be draped or swathed with silks, tulle, lace, or netting. The high, bulbous crowns offered space for pleating, beading, embroidery, or appliqué, and glorious trimmings of ribbon rosettes, silk flowers, and feathers. Spiky or soft bows could be attached to the side of the hat, giving it a slightly asymmetrical, graceful, and sophisticated look.

At her salon in the Place Vendôme, Maria Guy designed cloche hats which echoed the shape of World War I helmets and she trimmed them with loops and roses to add an impression *de hauteur* (height and grandeur) to the wearer. Suzanne Talbot, too, liked to make her clients look taller, and used her artistic skills by piling extra fabric on top of already deep crowns. Camille Roger rolled the brims up at the front, making them more flattering for older women. Madame Agnès,

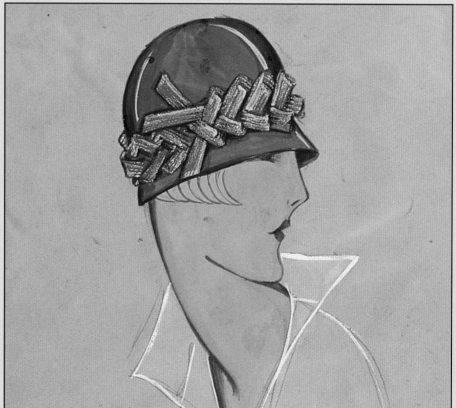

▌Stylish millinery design by Jeanne Lanvin. Charming and infinitely feminine cloche hats for the 1927/28 season, perfectly in tune with the new youthful fashion

1990-2000

1980-1990

1970-1980

1960-1970

1950-1960

1940-1950

1930-1940

1920-1930

1910-1920

1900-1910

▌*above* A variation of the classic cloche, small brimmed with a soft beret top
[courtesy of Pepin Press, Amsterdam]

▌*left* A glorious red winged hat from the Mauzan collection
[courtesy of Mr. Ronnie Barker]

▌*below* A classic cloche of the decade, circa 1925
[courtesy of Pepin Press, Amsterdam]

in the select Rue du Faubourg St-Honoré, had a reputation for her understated details and artistic style.

The 1925 Art Deco Exhibition in Paris was a major event influencing arts, crafts, and fashion design. Millinery was not excluded. Art Deco influences are clearly recognizable on many hats created in the mid-1920s. Art Deco shapes appeared in seam lines and on appliquéd materials, as well as on trimmings of decorative ornaments and jeweled hatpins.

The cloche attracted a lot of attention, but there were many other women's hat styles: closefitting turbans and *toques* and larger, soft cloches, all with very deep crowns, and worn pulled right down to eyebrow level. Glycerined ostrich feathers created a smoother, silky feeling and were sewn to some narrow cloche brims, creating a transparent fringe curtain, which flirtatiously concealed half the face, and gave a tantalising look of the *femme fatale*. Large pastel-colored, brimmed felt hats worn on

cool summer days to set off light, soft summer fur coats were considered to be the height of luxurious decadence and chic.

The most sought-after invitation was to be asked out to dine in a restaurant hat, which had a cartwheel brim full of feathers; or a swagged hat with streamers of feathers or flowers falling over one shoulder. Glamorous headdresses, perfect for dancing the Charleston, were decorated with beaded fringes, swaying feathers, or delicate flowers, symbolizing the crazy, exuberant, and

Jeanne Lanvin

FROM MILLINERY APPRENTICE TO DRESSING ARISTOCRACY

Jeanne Lanvin was a designer whose creations came straight from the heart. Her career started before the turn of the century and spanned well over four decades, up to her death in 1946. For half a century, she weathered the storms of two world wars, social upheavals, and changes in fashion, confident in her design ideas and the quality of her workmanship, something which was appreciated on both sides of the Atlantic. Her softly-colored, richly beaded and embroidered evening gowns and wedding dresses were works of art. The name Lanvin became synonymous with *haute couture* at its finest and her memory will live on in fashion history.

The story of Lanvin's life reads like a fairy tale. One of 10 children born to poor parents, she started at the very bottom of the ladder and built a *couture* empire of world repute. By 1938, she was honored with the *Légion d'Honneur*, she had married her daughter to a prince, and lived in a sumptuous Parisian mansion, decorated in her favorite hyacinth, a color which has since entered fashion dictionaries and is still referred to as Lanvin blue.

The young Jeanne began work at the age of 13 as a dressmaker's errand girl. Starting out as an apprentice to Madame Félix, a milliner in the Rue du Faubourg St-Honoré, Jeanne set up her own business—a millinery salon in an attic around the corner—at the age of 18. She had one client, little money, but great energy, and set about designing hats in her quiet, single-minded way, something for which she was known until the very end of her life.

The Lanvin wide cloche hat with fine edging and decorative details on the crown

▌A charming illustration for Lanvin's perfume *Arpège*, derived from the Italian musical term *arpeggio*, literally "in harmony." The scent was to be a celebration of her career and the social success of her adored daughter

▌A tight glittery cap for Twenties evening wear

▌A breton swept up high at the front with flame-shaped decorations framing the face

Always dressed elegantly in black with little touches of white, she projected an austere image and had little time for fashion gossip. Her twin passions were her work and her treasured daughter, Marguerite, who became the fairy princess of her dreams. Marguerite was Lanvin's only child, a pink and white beauty of exquisite grace, and a joy and ideal model for her mother. When Marguerite married and became the Countess Marie-Blanche de Polignac, the fairy tale came true.

Branching out into *couture* for children was a new and very successful idea, and led to further expansion into women's fashion, furs, and accessories. By the end of the 1920s, the Lanvin empire had expanded to include men's fashion, interior decor, and a range of perfumes.

Arpège, the perfume launched in 1927, was the crowning achievement of Lanvin's career and was dedicated to Marie-Blanche-Marguerite, who celebrated her thirtieth birthday that year. The perfume was a concoction of Bulgarian roses, jasmine from the south of France, honeysuckle, and lily of the valley—presented in a very elegant, round, black bottle, decorated with a golden image of Jeanne holding out her hands to her daughter.

Lanvin never made sensational headlines, nor did she claim to be at the forefront of fashion. According to one fashion critic her garments were "delightfully dated" but always new, fresh, and immensely desirable for young and mature women alike.

The House of Lanvin continued after her death and a succession of young designers were appointed to work in the spirit of the founder. Known as the *grande dame de couture*—the great lady of high fashion—Lanvin was inimitable and, sadly, the *couture* side of the Lanvin empire closed in 1993.

energetic lifestyle of the decade. Hats were regarded as the pinnacle of fashion and no woman would think of stepping out of the house without one.

New materials and novelties for trimmings were offered to milliners every season. Even though the basic hat shapes stayed much the same, fresh looks could be created by playing with different colors and combinations of fabrics and textures. The latest trends in fashion colors with romantic and exotic names were publicized in magazines and slavishly followed. In one season, hyacinth blue and jungle green might be the colors, in another, it could be scarlet or *bois de rose* (rosewood pink). *Tête de nègre* (dark brown) or burgundy could be the season's colors, giving a fresh look to the more classic soft beiges, browns, and grays so favored by Chanel. Suddenly one season, in 1927, everyone had to have yellow hats. Fashion became an exciting game and competition for style-conscious women, who wanted to be the first to be seen wearing the latest colors and styles.

Millinery, New York, and Hattie Carnegie

Contrary to Reboux's predictions about the demise of millinery, the 1920s went down in history as the decade of the hat. As with dress design, the center of fashion creation was Paris, from where ideas were exported all over Europe and the United States. Foreign buyers would arrive in France for the twice-yearly collections and select designs to be taken back to their countries. The power of buyers from the New York stores was legendary. For the Paris *couture* houses, the Americans were prized customers, who could make or break a season. Buyers chose designs to sell as Paris originals, or they imported samples to manufacture as Paris copies for a wider market.

This was also the system for buying hats and accessories. Hattie Carnegie was one of the legendary and powerful American buyers who were highly respected and greatly feared in Paris. Viennese by birth, Hattie started her career at the age of 15 by dressing hats for Macy's in New York. When she opened her

Vogue cover design for the July 11, 1928 issue entitled "At the Races"

own business, she changed her name to Carnegie, after millionaire Andrew Carnegie, the richest man in America. The Carnegie Look was publicized and retailed across the United States. Hattie Carnegie was not technically a designer and had never made any dresses, but her strong point was as a clever retailer with a great sense of style who always knew exactly what she could sell to her clientele in New York.

Millinery's answer to Hattie Carnegie was Lilly Daché who was an interesting example of a *midinette* from Paris turned powerful businesswoman in New York. Lilly learned the art of millinery from Caroline

A 1920s toque of pleated moquette [courtesy of Pepin Press, Amsterdam]

Jeweled diadem headbands and summer furs worn by the Rowe sisters, portraying the height of decadent luxury in the late 1920s

Madeleine Carroll in *Are Husbands Necessary?* wearing a demure blue jersey dress and hat designed by Lilly Daché

Reboux, before leaving for New York to sell hats at Macy's department store. Starting out by taking over a small hat shop on Broadway, she expanded her business and opened her famous salon in Madison Avenue. She could create hat designs out of almost anything and is known to have turned gold epaulettes from military uniforms into model hats. An excellent businesswoman, Lilly Daché expanded her business to Chicago, and returned regularly to Paris as a buyer, keeping up the exchange of hats between New York and Paris after World War I.

Hats were good business for American stores, because they made money and added chic, fun, and entertainment to fashion displays. Nathan Gibson Clark, the owner of a New York millinery business, sold only hats in his store and had a reputation for originality with his wisecracks and funny comments. Herman Patrick Tappé, designer-importer and the "Poiret" of New York, liked to dabble in millinery and is remembered for his outlandish hat designs, which he posed on his client's heads while reciting poetry and prose. Hats reflected the lighthearted mood of the 1920s, they never passed unnoticed, nor failed to draw attention and comment.

1990–2000
1980–1990
1970–1980
1960–1970
1950–1960
1940–1950
1930–1940
1920–1930
1910–1920
1900–1910

The Bowler

A Sign of its Time

Recognized as a quintessential symbol of Englishness, a **bowler** hat evokes images of a businessman striding purposefully through the City of London, briefcase and umbrella in hand, black like the bowler hat on his head.

During its 150-year history, the bowler hat has played so many different roles that it has become ingrained in people's minds all over the world. The instantly recognizable silhouette of this distinguished hat has illustrated lifestyles in nineteenth- and twentieth-century society and, like a comedian, it has played many roles making people laugh or cry. The bowler hat has been described, by turns, as stylishly sportive, lightheartedly funny, regimentally sober, modern and progressive, politically conservative, and comfortably reassuring. Chameleon-like, it has changed its image, adapting itself to place and time.

Mr William Bowler, after whom the hat is named, would not have expected fame or the future diversity of the hat, when he was asked to develop a new hat style in 1850 by James and George Lock of the gentlemen's hatters in London. In the Machine Age at the height of the Industrial Revolution, Mr Bowler set about perfecting an "iron hat." The brief, from English aristocrat William Coke II, later the Earl of Leicester, was to design a new headgear for gamekeepers on his country estate. The hat must be hard enough to protect the head from falling objects or injury in the event of being thrown off a horse. It also had to be low enough to make it unnecessary for the rider to duck to avoid the lower branches of trees. When Mr Coke went to London to collect the new hat, he traveled on the recently invented railway. This was perhaps a favorable omen for the hat, which became a city style; more suitable for riding "iron horses" (as locomotives were sometimes called) than the four-legged variety.

The first version of the hat—called a coke after the client who ordered it—took a while to perfect. The bowler was to be made from fine rabbit hair, felted to the highest specifications and stiffened with a mixture of **shellac** and mercury—a potent concoction that engulfed the Bowlers' South London factory with toxic fumes. The real test came when Mr Coke placed the hat on the floor and trod on it as hard as he could. Everyone held their breath, but the hat stayed intact. A clue to the rationale behind the hard hat is found in fashion historian Alison Lurie's book *The Language of Clothes*. In it, she observes that "traditionally whatever is worn on the head, is a sign of the mind beneath it."

The bowler hat, known in France as *chapeau melon* (melon hat) became a symbol of the modern, middle-class society which played such a key role in the social changes after World War I. In his book *The Man in the Bowler Hat*, Fred Miller Robinson describes the bowler as the symbol of the Industrial Revolution. It could be mass-produced, making it a "democratic" hat available to everyone and stylishly accessorized the modern lounge suits which had replaced the frock coat. The hat offered the wearer panache as well as protection and fitted with the new thinking that everybody could be a gentleman—if only he wore the right hat. Fred Miller Robinson sums it up perfectly when he says:

"The squire is a gentleman by birth, a Victorian solid citizen is a gentleman by virtue." Men's dress was democratized, and the concept of fashion as an imitation of the style of the upper classes was born. The chance for the bowler hat to cross the Atlantic came when it was seen at a fashionable English horserace meeting at Epsom that became known as the Derby (pronounced in Britain as "dahby"). The bowler's English style and aristocratic air did not compete with softer American hats, but took over the role that the formal top hat had filled before the Great War.

At the Museum of Modern Art in New York stands a bronze statue called *The Man in the Open Air*. The figure wears nothing but a distinctive bowler hat and a small bow on his chest. The sculpture was a gift to the museum from artist Ellie Nadelman, a Polish Jew who had fled to New York City in 1914. This slim, debonair, modern dandy seems at once strong and delicate, and gives an impression of assurance and gentle mockery. The bowler hat is worn very straight, and adds solidity to the slim and fluid figure. It represents the link between the old and the new world, modernity and convention.

The bowler's most famous screen appearance was in the silent films of Charlie Chaplin, who moved the hat firmly into the world of comedy. The oversized shoes and undersized hat, the badly fitting clothes and the cane were all part of the funny, but endearingly hopeless, tramp who was determined to become a gentleman. Charlie Chaplin aimed to make the bowler as much the tramp's crown as a symbol of a City of London gent. Following Chaplin's tradition came the famous pair of bowler-hatted comedians, Stan Laurel and Oliver Hardy, who used the hat to combine music hall tradition with comic sketches of social satire. The idea that a man needs a hat to preserve his dignity and that he only fits under his own hat, has significance and a deep duality of meaning which has made Laurel and Hardy films memorable testimonies of their time.

A battered bowler makes an appearance on the stage with the three tramps, Vladimir, Estragon, and Pozzo, in the play *Waiting for Godot* by Samuel Beckett. His portrayal of three Parisian *clochards* (tramps) is philosophical to some critics and trivial to others but the bowler hat is perhaps a good metaphor for the play itself—something which is everything and nothing.

More seriously, the bowler hat had a political role as the hat of the Weimar Republic during the 1920s. This period in history is well documented by English novelist Christopher Isherwood's autobiographical books, and was caricatured unforgettably by Liza Minnelli in the 1972 film *Cabaret*. The bowler was liked by Italian dictator Benito Mussolini during the 1930s. Adolf Hitler, hated the hat because it was worn by Jewish businessmen and it became known as *Judenstahlhelm* (Jewish steel helmet), outlawed in 1933 and used in posters of Nazi propaganda.

The bowler hat played a gangster role in Bertolt Brecht's *Threepenny Opera* in 1928. It was also worn by the violent and anarchistic hero of Stanley Kubric's 1971 *A Clockwork Orange*. Belgian illustrator and artist René Magritte painted images of fashion figures in bowler hats for advertisements and publicity work. Among his best known images are the mysterious bowler-hatted men facing backward, which, according to art historians show "the exchange between the respectable and the criminal." Magritte's *The Man in a Bowler Hat*, with the face of a man covered by a flying dove, exemplifies the anonymity conferred by the bowler hat, alerting us to the sort of man he might personify.

Black bowler hats were often worn by stockbrokers and people working in the City of London financial markets until well into the 1970s, and a few City lawyers still wear them today. The bowler hat has had a colorful history and will certainly never be forgotten but in a decade or so it might well gain a new popularity through another quick-change act.

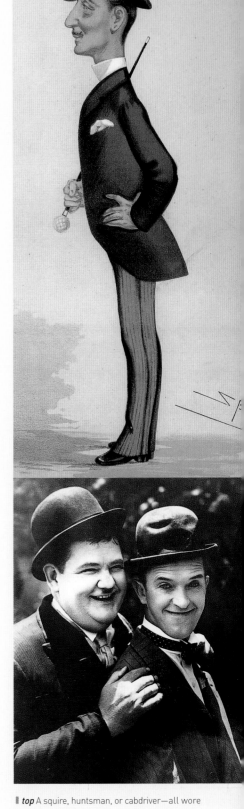

top A squire, huntsman, or cabdriver—all wore the "iron hat" which was to democratize men's fashion

above Laurel and Hardy, a bowler-hatted duo of unforgettable comedians steeped in the music hall tradition

far left Charlie Chaplin in his role as the tramp in 1915 made the bowler hat his trademark. City gentleman degraded to tramp, or tramp turned gentleman—who knows?

A Return to Sobriety

T OWARD THE END OF THE 1920s, THERE WERE SIGNS THAT THE bubble of fun and prosperity would burst, but nothing had prepared the American people for the Wall Street Crash on October 29, 1929. The financial catastrophe not only shook the foundations of the American Dream, but also sent a tidal wave of depression over Europe and the rest of the world.

By 1933, 13 million Americans, one quarter of the total work force, were unemployed. These figures were similar over the Atlantic, in Britain and across Europe. The Great Depression swept away much of the material and social progress of the Twenties decade plunging millions of people into hardship and poverty.

The whole idea and concept of capitalism and materialism was questioned by the younger generation, who fell victim to political propaganda from the extreme right and left. Meanwhile, Germany elected Adolf Hitler and the National Socialist Party in 1933 and the Soviet Union was ruled by communism under the heavy iron fist of secretary Joseph Stalin.

Reactions to the economic crisis sparked off changes in attitudes and morality, which in turn had an impact on the role of women in society. After the financial crash, fashion had to be leaner, economical, and conservative. To advertise emancipation was considered offensive and the rebellious, boyish looks of the 1920s were swiftly replaced by much softer, figure-hugging styles. In the early 1930s, the ideal female shape was elegant with slender hips and feminine curves accentuated by soft flowing skirts at mid-calf length. High-heeled shoes lifted the whole silhouette. Face and hair were well-groomed, with pencil thin eyebrows, pale make-up, and a discreetly waved platinum blonde *coiffure*. According to the fashion pages of *Vogue*, the look to aim for was

Greta Garbo

MESMERIZING MYSTIQUE

Many things have been said about Garbo. She was supposed to have been sensual, glacial, spiritual, down-to-earth, emotional, detached, difficult, and mysterious. Often called the face of the century, she had an enigmatic image which reflected the glamor as well as the unease of the 1930s. Garbo epitomized the duality of extravagance and seriousness, which was so evident in the years leading up to World War II.

Adored by her many fans, who called themselves Garbomaniacs, she became an international obsession during the 1930s, arousing feelings of true passion as well as hate. Through it all, she strode aloof, strong-willed, and seemingly indifferent to the fuss around her. In a profile in the *New Yorker* magazine in 1931, journalist Virgilia Peterson describes the actress arriving at a Hollywood party: "Miss Greta Garbo was announced. She came in wearing a beret over her straight blonde hair, a tailored suit, a man's shirt, and a tie, and a pair of flat-heeled shoes. When the guests saw her face, their talk abruptly died away. She sat alone and silent, unwilling or unable to share any social responsibility. Garbo had frozen the evening."

Her glacial aloofness turned into hot passion on the screen, mesmerizing audiences. Queen Christina was one of her classic roles in the film of the same name in which Sweden's seventeenth-century monarch gave up her throne for love. At the end of the film, Christina sails into exile. In total solitude she watches the Swedish coastline recede. The scene didn't leave many dry eyes in the audience. The image of Garbo's face with her serious, expressive eyes and long eyelashes throwing shadows on her cheeks is unforgettable.

▌ Greta Garbo's unforgettable face framed with a theatrically ornate and jeweled millinery creation

▌ *opposite* Vogue cover March 17, 1937: "Rejoicing in spring and summer fashion with toques scattered all over with silk flowers like a Garden of Eden"

Greta Garbo was also a fashion icon and the ideal of the romantic woman in the 1930s. Her fashion style was widely imitated. The **slouch hats** that mysteriously shadowed her face have entered fashion vocabulary as the Garbo look. Her enigmatic and sensual style of dress has been reinvented by many designers over the years, but all attempts were only pale imitations of her unique style.

In the 1940s, desperate to escape the unbearable glare of publicity, Garbo retired from the movies. This only increased her fame and fanned the obsession of the public and the media who wanted to discover the secret of this mysterious woman. Beautiful and glamorous, Greta Garbo looked at the world with gloomy eyes and, like the Sphinx of ancient mythology, she never revealed her secret. Her aim was to be a Hollywood star, but having achieved it, she wanted to escape from it all.

Icon of the decade

Claude Saint-Cyr

MILLINER TO THE QUEEN

Claude Saint-Cyr, often referred to as *la grande Claude Saint-Cyr*, deserves a special mention, because of her revered place in the illustrious circle of 1930s Parisian milliners. Starting her fashion career at Patou, Claude Saint-Cyr went to London to learn millinery, and in a dramatic, *avant-garde* gesture she changed her name from Simone to the androgynous "Claude." A beautiful and intelligent young woman with flair and imagination, it was not long before French *Vogue* was inviting her to be photographed in her own hats. Just as with Chanel, it was the man in Claude Saint-Cyr's life—a successful businessman who loved skiing, aviation, and driving a Bugatti—who helped her to set up her own business in the Rue du Faubourg St-Honoré. The salon was an oasis of sophisticated, calm elegance. Claude hated fuss and disorder and treated her hats as if they were roses in need of care and artful arrangement. An undisputed master of clean lines, perfect proportions, and harmonious design, she was convinced that a hat should naturally place itself on a woman's head and make her feel good as well as look beautiful. Cool, orderly, and sophisticated, Claude was a perfect symbol of the 1930s and her classic, stylish hats have become collectors' items.

During the 1940s, her clientele expanded to include the Duchess of Windsor, Lady Mountbatten, and other members of the British Royal Family. At the beginning of the following decade, Norman Hartnell, who was responsible for designing Queen Elizabeth II's clothes, encouraged Claude Saint-Cyr to open a workshop in London.

On several occasions, she was summoned to design hats for Queen Elizabeth, wife of George VI, and the Royal Princesses. When Princess Elizabeth was crowned Queen Elizabeth II in 1952, it was Claude Saint-Cyr who was called in to sort out a problem with the crown. The ancient crown of St. Edward, worn by previous kings, was much too large for Her Royal Highness's head. Bobo, as the Queen later affectionately called Claude, devised a small, round, velvet cushion, which was sewn into the crown to help it fit and balance. Fortunately, there were fewer problems when the Queen's sister, Princess Margaret called on Claude to arrange her wedding coronet and veil.

A legend in hat history, Claude Saint-Cyr will always be remembered for her elegant hats that combined French chic and English classicism.

Vogue's spring report on "high-hatting" for 1935 suggested: "there's always something young and jaunty about a tall hat with feathers"

Hats Add Spice to a 1930s Wardrobe

For daywear, sobriety was the key theme. Sports clothes were practical, slightly masculine, and always meticulously tailored. Buys for a new wardrobe might be: shirtwaist and coat dresses, soft, bias-cut skirts, lingerie blouses, fitted or boxy coats, tailored trousers, sailor's jumpers, and boy-scout shorts. Accessories provided light relief to this somber style of dressing. Hats contributed a little spice and wit and offered an opportunity for adding an individual note.

Milliners followed the mood of the times and created curvaceous styles, romantically trimmed, and worn far forward and tilted over one eye. A soft face veil often completed the picture. Brims became flatter, and crowns lower, until the totally flat "pancake panama" became a hit in 1933. Height was added again when Madame Agnès created the *coup de foudre* (literally "a thunderbolt" or "love at first sight") described by *Vogue* as the skyscraper model. French hat designer Maria Guy, whom *Vogue* called "one of the bright minds of the millinery divinity," also contributed to "high-hatting." She designed tall toques like the Cossack cap and the **fez**, adding even more height with topknots and feathers.

The sleek, upswept hairstyles accentuated a beautiful neckline and went hand in hand with sophisticated hats. Musing on the relationship between hair and hats, American *Vogue* noted that: "The first glimpse of hair beneath a forward-riding *chapeau* gives a rather startled feeling, but is very smart and very, very new!" In a further issue of *Vogue*: "On the other hand, those little silly hats that you see lunching at the Colony, show curls, not wopses of curls, but little soft ringlets, progressing higher as hats become more determined to Reveal All..."

Most flattering of all were the flowered toques with masses of violets, roses, or lilies of the valley piled up high for a most romantic and feminine look. *Vogue* described one of these *bijou* hats: "Velvet petals scattered all over a wickedly innocent, little turban called "Garden of Eden"—high and square at the back, but kept small and light

"a mixture of a fashionable beauty and a Byzantine Madonna, with the added grace of a white lily."

Women's lives were again focused on home, social entertainment, and frivolities, and there was a nostalgic yearning for luxuries and the precise social etiquette of the prewar years. Society women took infinite time to plan and refine an elegant, expensive, but economical wardrobe, which was seen as a lasting investment. An afternoon dress was one of the most important items and had to be discreetly luxurious, in subdued colors and bias-cut georgette or crepe. The skirt was flared at the bottom and hemmed at exactly 12 inches above the ground. For dancing in the early evening, ankle length was required. Full evening dresses had to be toe length and could be accessorized with a short cape of fluffy fur and long, satin gloves. The look was tall and slender, and emphasized the figure, which was kept in trim by exercising or, for women with a not-so-perfect figure, by wearing a soft corset called a *maillot*, a kind of body stocking.

1990–2000

1980–1990

1970–1980

1960–1970

1950–1960

1940–1950

1930–1940

1920–1930

1910–1920

1900–1910

Lilly Daché

HATS IN MANHATTAN

An example of successful transatlantic exchange was Parisian milliner Lilly Daché, who had set herself up in business in New York. The Daché hat emporium grew so successful that she took over a whole building in 1938, installing her own penthouse with seven floors of hats below. On the first floor was a round salon with leopard-print sofas; a silver fitting-room for blonde clients and a gold one for brunettes. Among the best known Daché hats were the **profile** shape that framed the face, smart turbans, **snoods**, and evening hats decorated with silk flowers.

In the 1940s, the business expanded to Chicago, and dresses and other accessories were added to the Daché range. Like *haute couture* houses in Paris, perfumes were created and marketed under names such as *Drifting* and *Dashing*. Lilly Daché published her autobiography in the Fifties called *Talking Through My Hats*.

❚ The 1930s "profile hat," a favorite of Lilly Daché and her American clientele

1990–2000

1980–1990

1970–1980

1960–1970

1950–1960

1940–1950

1930–1940

1920–1930

1910–1920

1900–1910

by a fold flattened down over the forehead."
Another little gem called *Ne m'oubliez pas*
(remember me), which looked like a
handkerchief folded around gathered
flowers, was recommended for wear on
special afternoons, preferably with a Vionnet
designer dress, gloves of satin or *peau d'ange*
(angel skin), and an antelope bag.

Milliners also offered large cartwheel
hats, slouchy Greta Garbo fedoras, and
cache-misère turbans—essential for the days
when hair just had to be hidden away.
Designer Elsa Schiaparelli liked to add a
surreal touch to her accessories, creating
witty and daring hats which were a special
favorite of the Honorable Mrs Reginald
Fellowes, a society beauty of American
ancestry known as Daisy in exclusive
international social circles. Toward the end
of the 1930s, with a sense of almost uncanny
premonition, milliners created hat styles
which leaned towards military looks with
tricorns, bicorns, and peak caps.

The hat design center was still Paris,
where important fashion houses like Reboux,
Agnès, and Paulette employed up to 300
appreteuses (milliners) and *vendeuses*
(saleswomen) each. The large salons were
subdivided into *ateliers* (workshops), each
headed by a *première*, who was always
addressed as Madame. The *première* was
assisted by a *seconde*, also called Madame,
and surrounded by a team of between 10 and
20 milliners, as well as two apprentices. The
more senior apprentice was called *apprentie
en chef* (head apprentice) and the younger
one, who was at the very bottom of the
hatmaking hierarchy, was called simply
la nouvelle (the new girl).

The first two years of an apprenticeship
were spent serving the milliners, by running
around for bits of materials and trimmings,
fetching the right colored threads, and
passing pins during fittings. Two years of
learning *avec les yeux* (by watching) was
considered the essential basis for learning
the milliner's craft. All Parisian milliners,
even the *petites mains* (helpers), considered
themselves superior to the girls in the
dressmaking and tailoring *ateliers*. Girls from
the millinery workshops were always well
dressed and meticulously groomed. They
loved fun, flirting, and wit. It was said in

Designs by the trio of Parisian "millinery divinity," Caroline Reboux, Agnès, and Maria Guy

couture circles that while dressmakers
worked for their living, milliners spent their
money on face powder and lipstick. The
rumor also ran that these young ladies were
very much appreciated by rich gentlemen
with wives and houses in the country.

In addition to the well-known hat salon,
Maison Reboux, there was a whole host of
"divine" milliners in Paris, as American *Vogue*
noted in 1933. They all had special styles
associated with their names. Maria Guy
could translate exotic **chéchias** into
sensational hats, Suzy was acclaimed for her
black satin dinner *toques*, Rose Valois for
flowery, romantic hats, and Rose Descat
for chic, little Panamas. La Maison J. Suzanne
Talbot upheld the reputation for theatrical

creations, while Agnès designed Parisian
tricorns covered in little flowers. Louise
Bourbon reinvented the fez as a fashion item,
and Madame Paulette, who opened her salon
in 1939, was to become the queen of the
turban. Some *haute couture* houses like
Patou, Chanel, Lanvin, and Molyneux had
world-renowned millinery workshops. Each
atelier created hats within the fashion style
or look of the house, known as *la griffe*.

The Rise of American Fashion Design

The economic depression and the financial
restraints of the 1930s put expensive Parisian
designs beyond the reach of many people.

Elsa Schiaparelli

SHOCKING PINK, SURREALISM, AND SHOES ON HEADS

Hated by Coco Chanel and adored by Salvadore Dali Elsa Schiaparelli dressed Hollywood stars Greta Garbo, Marlene Dietrich, and Joan Crawford and took Paris by storm. Born in Rome, she counted Renaissance architecture among her childhood influences and antiquity as the inspiration for her teenage poems. In London, she found spiritualism and a husband, was excited by skyscrapers and modernism in New York, but finally settled in Paris, the city where she had always felt at home.

After her marriage failed, accompanied by her sick daughter and a woman friend, Schiaparelli arrived penniless in the French capital in 1922. "I owe my success to poverty and Paris," she declared in an interview in 1954, "Poverty forced me to work, and Paris gave me the courage to do it." The first step on the road to fame and fortune was a black sweater with an inset white bow that she had designed for herself for a skiing holiday. Friends admired it so much that quickly a team of Armenian knitters were set to work in an attic on the Left Bank.

The resulting *trompe l'oeil* (trick of the eye) sweater collection was a great success and clients from far and wide flocked to "the little woman with her sweaters" at the Rue de la Paix. Schiaparelli's meteoric rise and expansion into dress design occurred when she moved the business into a magnificent house on the Place Vendôme in 1934. A year later, a London salon was opened. Her dynamic energy, surreal wit, her broad-shouldered and perfectly tailored suits, and above all her invention of the color "shocking pink" have all been debated, celebrated, and immortalized in countless stories about Schiaparelli.

Shocking Pink was also the name of the Schiaparelli perfume, for which she designed a bottle in the shape of a woman's body, modeling it on Mae West's vital statistics.

Schiaparelli loved to shock and had enormous fun designing hats. Her philosophy was that a flattering hat was great on a beautiful woman, but a crazy hat could be a defense against insecurity for someone not so attractive. As a child, she had practiced this theory on herself, decorating her face with flowers and thinking that their loveliness would rub off on her, making her look pretty, too. Hats lend themselves to fantasy and were a favourite medium for creativity for Schiaparelli, who unleashed all her artistic imagination, drawn from cubism, futurism, and surrealism. She created toy hats, pincushion hats, large pie-pan hats with long stemmed lilies, berets that could be transformed into French judge's toques, Russian crowns, and forward-leaning **skylarkers**.

▌Surreal designs of shoe hats by Elsa Schiaparelli, 1937

▌Schiaparelli's romantic fantasy flower garden hat

Seashell hats were created out of layered and pleated organza, others were decorated with dyed pink horsehair, fruit, grass, or vegetables. Pencils replaced hatpins, in case the wearer needed to write something down! She introduced the crushed fedora look, which she called the Tangle. Straw hats were fitted with vanity cases inside the crowns and for one collection, velvet monk's cowls were made with flaps that could be tied up and transformed into a turban.

There were no limits to the materials Schiaparelli used for making hats. It could be black, shiny patent leather, saffron yellow or Tunisian blue satin, but it could also be newspaper, plastic propellers, chimney pots, or bird cages with singing canaries inside. The hat follies had no limits. The 1935 collection even included a futuristic television hat.

Schiaparelli hats were a delight for the media who sent reports and pictures around the world, causing shrieks of laughter on both sides of the Atlantic. She created an upside-down shoe hat in 1937 which was said to have been worn by socialite Daisy Fellowes, but a daring beret in the shape of a mutton chop, made of patent leather with white lacy frill over the bone, was only worn by Elsa Schiaparelli herself.

After France capitulated to the Nazis in 1940, Schiaparelli left Paris for the United States. When World War II ended, she returned but was never able to regain her influential prewar position. The mood and appetite for eccentric and outrageous design had diminished, and Schiaparelli, who had provided "daring, playfulness, and fun," as stated by *Vogue* editor Diana Vreeland, did not fit into the conformist and conventional atmosphere of the 1950s.

Chic Spanish matador-inspired hat with a flat crown and fur edging

1990-2000
1980-1990
1970-1980
1960-1970
1950-1960
1940-1950
1930-1940
1920-1930
1910-1920
1900-1910

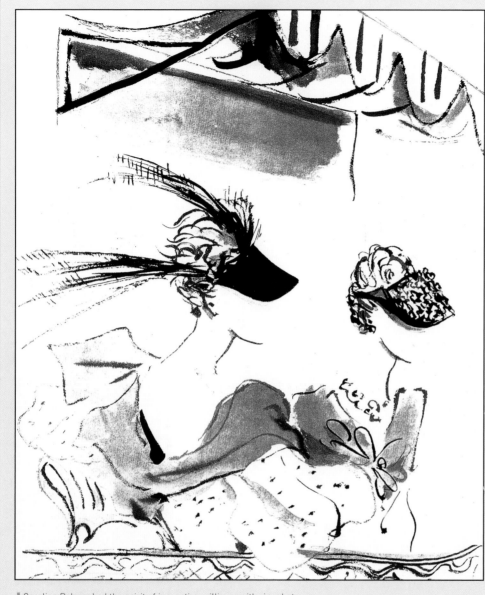

❙ Caroline Reboux had the spirit of innovative millinery with visor hats

❙ *top* Rose Valois invented divine topknots to add height, decorating her hats with upright loops and stiffened bows

❙ *above* Mrs Wallis Simpson, just before her wedding to the Duke of Windsor, the former uncrowned King Edward VIII. Edward abdicated on December 10, 1936, forsaking his crown and kingdom to marry the woman he loved

In America and in Britain, young designers began to develop home-grown fashion. Prestigious stores in New York, including Saks Fifth Avenue, Bonwit Teller, and Bergdorf Goodman, were still dependent on Paris for originals, adaptations, duplication, and copying, but they started to gain confidence in American designers.

Main Rousseau Bocher, a young student in New York, found fame under the name Mainbocher and was the first American designer to open a *couture* house in Paris. He was the favorite designer of Wallis Simpson, the future Duchess of Windsor; his designs complementing perfectly her neat, slimline elegance. Restrained, sophisticated simplicity was the key in his salon. Mainbocher's models were always dressed in neat, black, bias-cut dresses, accessorized with three rows of pearls and classic court shoes. "The things that Mainbocher can do with black are almost phenomenal," American *Vogue* noted in 1933. He was the declared "genius of black," designing neat, elegant dresses, bolero jackets, and unfussy, sophisticated hats.

When she married the Duke of Windsor in 1936, Wallis Simpson chose Mainbocher to make her wedding outfit. The fabric had to be dyed a special shade of blue, which is recorded in fashion history as Wallis blue. Mainbocher never dictated loud, ostentatious fashion; he stood for the elegant simplicity that was also the Duchess of Windsor's hallmark. His designs and her looks exuded refinement with great sophistication and were always "underwhelmingly" dazzling.

Mainbocher was editor of French *Vogue* before he opened his salon in Paris, and felt very settled in France. After the German takeover of Paris in the early years of World War II, he was forced to return to the United States, where he established a *couture* house in New York's Fifth Avenue.

The Trilby

A SOFT HAT FOR HARD MEN

A trilby is a man's soft felt hat, closely related to the larger fedora style, with a low, indented crown, and a neat ribbon as a trimming. Both hats have literary origins and wearers have often formed affectionate attachments to these hats, in a way that is quite different to the topper or the bowler which were worn as a status symbol rather than as a personal statement.

Was it the softness of the felt that molded itself so well to the shape of the head, or was it the three fingerspan that dented the crown that gave it such an individual note? The trilby is a very personal hat, comfortable and protective against the rain, always in subdued shades of gray or brown, blending in with the crowd—the required look for men's clothing in the democratic postwar age. The fashion had come from America and was worn by young *avant-garde* Bohemians, after the turn of the century, as a sign of liberation from the stiff, hard hats of the past. Symbolically, they wanted to shed the stiff, authoritarian image of their fathers and grandfathers.

Interestingly, the hat is named after the female heroine in a 1889 melodrama of the same name by George du Maurier. The British writer was a master of satire who loved to excite his readers with stories about love, sacrifice, and man's dominance over women. His novel *Trilby* is set in a social background of barbarians, Bohemians, and the *bourgeoisie*. Trilby O'Ferrall, a pretty Irish girl, earns her living by being an artist's model in Paris and, in the stage play of the book, wears the soft, indented hat so familiar to us. She is loved by a young English painter, but falls slowly under the mesmeric spell of Svengali, a German-Polish musician, who trains her as a singer and helps her become a famous performer, by exploiting her popularity. Such is Svengali's power over Trilby that she loses her singing voice when he dies and becomes ill, soon following her demonic mentor to the grave.

The book was serialized in *Harper's New Monthly Magazine*, creating great suspense among its readers, libel actions, and an outcry from the public because of references to nudity as well as racial aspects. In an 1895 dramatization, actor Herbert Beerbohm Tree's powerful portrayal of Svengali on stage produced wide acclaim for the play and a lasting fashion for his victim's headgear.

In the 1930s, the trilby moved to the heads of gangsters, racketeers, crooked gamblers, and colorful characters like those in Damon Runyon's 1932 novel *Guys and Dolls*. Early in his career, Runyon was a crime reporter and modeled all his characters on real criminals that he had encountered. The musical by Frank Loesser based on the book offers a walk on the shady side of 1930s New York. Where would colorful "operators" like Sky Masterson, Nathan Detroit, and Nicely-Nicely Johnson be without their trilbies?

In gangland, clothes and fashion are a symbol of status and money. A screen gangster is never seen without a trenchcoat, a hat, and a cigarette to give him masculinity and credibility. In her book *Undressing the Cinema*, writer Stella Bruzzi elaborates: "Gangsters are not only men of action, but also men of fashion, and the hat is essential to that image." In *Miller's Crossing*, by the Coen brothers, the hat takes over the story, getting lost and being found again; being gambled away and knocked off in a fight. The hero has a nightmare about the hat being blown away, but luckily it comes back. He can cope with almost any kind of difficulty, except losing his hat.

French actor Alain Delon plays an assassin in the 1967 film *The Samurai*. He always appears in trenchcoat and trilby, which he adjusts carefully in the mirror everytime he goes out. The hat is his protection and security, making him anonymous and identifiable at the same time; it is the armor that shields him from the enemy. Even when the assassin is shot and bleeding through his trenchcoat, he is still wearing his trilby hat, although it has slipped to the back of his head. Even a chase scene through the Paris subway, sees the hat staying firmly on his head.

Le Doulos is another French gangster film made in the 1960s and directed by Jean-Pierre Melville and starring Jean-Paul Belmondo. The French title comes from a slang word, *doulos*, which means "hat" and also "police informer." In the final scene of the movie, the hero, dying from a gunshot wound, staggers, checks his appearance in a nearby car mirror, raises his hat, and falls dead. As Melville once said: "Perfection is to attain immortality—then die."

Since the trilby became associated with disreputable elements in society, it was perhaps inevitable that it would find its way to another head—the newspaper reporter's. In the world of black-and-white American "B" movies unshaven, trilby-hatted figures lurch into phone booths, shove in a couple of dimes, and shout, "Gimme rewrite!" For decades afterward, when television dramas required a unsavory reporter, they made the actor wear a trilby. Miss Trilby O'Ferrall, one suspects, would not have been amused.

▌*opposite* Frank Sinatra, American idol and singer, wore his trilby "his way." Worn jovially on the back of his head, the hat represented his image of easy-going heartthrob, which helped sell his records all over the world

▌*above* French film star and sixties idol Alain Delon plays an assassin in *The Samurai*. A trenchcoat with deep pockets conceals his gun, while a trilby worn low and shading the face was the essential attire of survival for any self-respecting gangster on stage or screen

▌*below* Soft hats for hard men—an advertisement for menswear in the Thirties

Knapp-Felt
SOFT HATS *for* MEN

Knapp-Felt DeLuxe, Six Dollars
Knapp-Felt, Four Dollars

War and Renewal

IN AN HISTORIC RADIO BROADCAST ON SEPTEMBER 3, 1939, BRITISH prime minister Neville Chamberlain announced to a stunned nation that Britain was at war with Germany. By the middle of June, 1940, Hitler's troops had marched into Paris, and France had capitulated to the Germans, forming a collaborationist government at Vichy, a town in central France. The United States entered World War II after the Japanese bombed Pearl Harbor on December 7, 1941. The unthinkable had happened. Just over 20 years after the horrors of World War I, a new conflict had broken out. Nations all around the globe were engulfed in terror and untold human suffering. This second world war was not greeted with enthusiasm like the war in 1914, but with fear, and the mood was of sobriety, austerity, and economic caution.

Wartime Wear

As always, fashion reflected the mood of the time, which was sobriety, practicality, and restraint. The feminine frivolities of the 1930s were over. Shortages of paper, fabric, and leather, as well as general clothes rationing, affected everyone and continued right through the war and the years after. In 1947, the news of fresh, feminine styles, called the New Look, filtered through from Paris and heralded a new sense of luxury.

The "make do and mend" wartime years were restricting for fashion designers, but did not stop the desire for femininity and fashion. Clothes rationing encouraged women to dress with imagination and ingenuity on a very limited budget. Defiant fashion magazines encouraged women to buy "smart stand-bys,"

[Ulrike Koeb, Vienna]

▌ Feathered cap by Adele List, created in 1951 and worn by Viennese society lady, Marianne Schönberg, who was an ardent admirer of Adele List's creations. Private collector's piece

support the fight for democracy was by buying a British suit. According to *Vogue*, this was "as much a contribution to British defense as a sum of money." *Vogue* continued dramatically: "A new sweater puts another nail in a plane for Britain!"

After the German occupation of France, Paris *couture* was no longer available in the free world and American fashion focused on home-grown products, giving American designers, previously overshadowed by Paris, a real chance to show their talents. Mainbocher had returned to New York and, encouraged by his success, many new designers established themselves. Charles James gained a reputation for sculptured evening gowns, Norman Norell created a sequinned, glamor look with classic lines, and Claire McCardell, the creator of the all-American casual style, made dresses out of surplus military balloon cloth. Young American designers created elegant, convenient, and affordable clothes and built the foundations for the postwar explosion in American fashion.

John Frederics, the first American master milliner, headed a list of New York hatmakers who started to manufacture less expensive lines. His millinery team created an inexpensive line of hats labeled "John Frederic Charmers." Lilly Daché followed this example and expanded her collection with a range of Dachettes. Sally Victor had a ready-to-wear line called Sally V, and Mr. John, who had set up on his own after leaving John Frederics, produced his own less expensive line of hats under the label of Mr. John Juniors. The trend in ready-to-wear hat production was followed after the war by Otto Lucas, who created a million-dollar business by expanding the American idea across the Atlantic in London.

In France, the fashion scene during the war years was very different. French women were not allowed to wear uniforms of any kind, because they could have been associated with the war effort or the resistance movement. Despite German directives against makeup and dyed hair, women dressed as extravagantly and as femininely as they could. People felt that the rationing of clothing could only benefit the German occupiers and that it was much

to "wear washables," and to dance for charity, in addition to teaching practicalities like how to reline old coats; how to make felt boots from old sweaters, and giving general advice on how to "knit your own way to chic." British *Vogue* published regular useful suggestions in its columns like "Shophounds on a budget" and "Shophound chat at the fireside." These gave hints on how to look smart while doing housework such as "dusting your home in a homemade drawstring snood."

Women were required to keep the homefires burning, take on men's work, cope with shortages and bombings, and look pretty when their men came home on leave. Some puritans tried to ban makeup, but women ignored this, clinging to lipstick, powder, hair, and hats as a last feminine indulgence. The ideal look was "discreetly understated with a touch of romance." What better way to achieve this than with a groomed face and a lovely hat.

Across the Atlantic there was a feeling of solidarity for the war effort in Britain. American *Vogue* encouraged their readers to make war contributions by buying British goods. One way that women could help

Mae West

SEX APPEAL WITH WIT

Yet another aspect of womanhood was represented by Mae West in the 1940s. Discovered by Hollywood at the mature age of 40, she starred in *Night After Night*, followed by *I'm No Angel*, and other hit movies during the 1930s. Portraying sexy, witty, and slightly coarse heroines, Mae West improvised many of the saucy one-liners for which she became known. Her explicit wit was frowned upon by the censors and her seductive clothing and hats accentuated her personality and helped convey the *vaudeville* image she liked to portray.

After starring with W.C. Fields in *My Little Chickadee* in 1940, she more or less gave up cinema and returned to a career in Broadway shows and touring nightclubs around the world. Mae West was a born "baby vamp" and a nightclub singer on and off screen. She played her last vamp role in 1978, two years before her death at the age of 85.

Ingrid Bergman

PURITY AND WOMANLY CHARM

Like Greta Garbo, Ingrid Bergman was Swedish and a natural beauty, shining with inner emotions, without needing to make dramatic gestures or wear much makeup. Adored by the public, she always portrayed a good woman of respectable desirability, ideal for the war years in the early 1940s.

Making her Hollywood debut in *Intermezzo* in 1939, Ingrid Bergman found fame when she replaced Hedy Lamarr in *Casablanca*, co-starring with Humphrey Bogart. About love, loyalty, and French resistance against the Nazis, the story is set in French-ruled Morocco, over which looms the shadow of the German-controlled Vichy government in France.

Bergman seduced her men with sincere and mature charm. Her wardrobe reinforced that image with elegant hats worn like halos at the back of her head, or slightly shadowing her face. In *For Whom the Bell Tolls*, another story of passionate love set in a background of political conflict, Bergman was unforgettable. After winning an Oscar for her 1944 performance in *Gaslight* with French actor Charles Boyer, she was nominated the nation's top dramatic star, but was blacklisted by the press when her private life did not match her pure image portrayed on screen. Like Garbo, Ingrid Bergman left Hollywood at the height of her career and moved to Italy to be with Italian director Roberto Rossellini and her daughter, Isabella.

PICTURE **POST**

EASTER BONNETS
See page 24

HULTON'S
NATIONAL
WEEKLY

TOM WINTRINGHAM ON PLANNING A
CONTINENTAL LANDING 4ᴰ

APRIL 24, 1943   Vol. 19. No. 4

▌ *Picture Post* cover, 1943, featuring one of the exotic Easter hats by milliner Rose Bertin. Easter bonnets were a craze in the 1940s and millinery design competitions became a tradition on both sides of the Atlantic. This cherry-laden model is an example of a hat created to symbolize gaiety and spring

Military millinery influences of the late war years; a victorious velvet cap trimmed with pheasant quills, 1949, and a stylish felt beret created in 1944

1990–2000

1980–1990

1970–1980

1960–1970

1950–1960

1940–1950

1930–1940

1920–1930

1910–1920

1900–1910

better to keep the French fashion industry busy and alive. A defiant group of French designers prevented Goebbels, the Nazi Minister for Propaganda, from closing down Parisian *haute couture* and relocating the whole business to Berlin and Vienna. Paris *couture* designed for French customers and for the wives of the German occupying forces; businesses that refused to serve Germans were closed down.

The women of Paris liked to tease the German occupying forces by wearing garish colours, short skirts, and excessively high hats, decorated with ostentatious trimmings. Colorful dress was a sign of free spirit and was a way of expressing a nation's pride and protest against foreign rule. After the liberation of Paris in August, 1944, the frivolous look disappeared and clothes and fashion came into line with the American and British attitudes that ostentatious dress was wasteful and unpatriotic.

Hats to Brighten Wartime Gloom

During the war years, most fashion luxuries disappeared, except for hats which took on a cheerleader role and raised female spirits. Hats were described as a "traditional tonic," which could "pull off a transformation of scene, single-handedly," as British *Vogue* wrote in 1941. Women could choose between straight *canotiers* (boaters), upturned **Breton** sailors' hats, boatshaped brims, pancake berets, doll's miniature hats, **postillions**, extravagant cartwheels, and demure snoods. Turbans were recommended as most practical headgear, "for when tough winds blow and taxis are scarce, you remain imperturbably groomed."

Supplies of straw had stopped completely, and the hat industry was running short of other materials and trimmings. Milliners turned the shortages into new

opportunities, using stiffened cottons, knitted fabrics, and scraps of all sorts to make and decorate hats. *Vogue* reported in an article called *Hat Matters* that "milliners had made ladies' hats newer, more varied, and more charming than we could have hoped." Hats provided relief during the gloomy, drab years of the early 1940s and helped to brighten the mood of the nation. Their role was to "enliven faces which had become too serious," and so hats became morale boosters as well as expressions of individuality.

Danish milliner Aage Thaarup, working in London, never missed an opportunity for fun and wit. He designed a unique and elaborate hat combining a gas mask, a poker dice set, and a brandy flask in a case, and covered it all with clippings from his favorite poems as a trimming. In America, Elizabeth Arden countered wartime worries by designing an exquisite waterproof

Marlene Dietrich

THE BLUE ANGEL

Marlene Dietrich's career had taken off during the 1930s, when she made six films in as many years under the direction of Josef Von Steinberg. The first and the most famous was *The Blue Angel* in 1930. The movie, based on a story by novelist Heinrich Mann, was about a respected elderly academic who falls disastrously in love with Lola, a bewitching nightclub singer. Dietrich's husky voice singing *Falling in love again* echoed in many ears for years to come.

In *Morocco*, Dietrich's portrayal of Amy, a cabaret singer who dressed in a man's tail coat and top hat, became an unforgettable image of sexual ambiguity. In the title role of *Shanghai Lily*, Steinberg had her wrapped erotically in feather boas and veils, and Dietrich's extravagant costumes in *Blonde Venus* showed off her irresistible seductiveness and sex appeal.

Marlene Dietrich was heralded as the new Garbo and her image of a *femme fatale* who ensnares men stayed with her all her life. Her popularity as an actress took a downturn in the 1940s, so she started a new career as a cabaret singer, entertaining United States troops during World War II and helping anti-Nazi propaganda in her native Germany.

▌ *left* Dietrich, the queen of Hollywood, looking regal in a glittering gown and richly-embroidered toque with fan-shaped crown

▌ *opposite* Wartime fashion icon Marlene Dietrich, wearing a lush fur-trimmed wraparound coat with a small draped cap decorated with a high top knot and trimmed with extravagant feather *aigrettes*

Adele List

VIENNESE DEDICATION TO MILLINERY

*A*mongst milliners, Adele List was an unusual character. Not interested in fashion, she developed her craft on an intellectual basis. Once when she was asked why she made such technically complicated hats, her reply was: "Because I am a religious person and everything I do is an obligation and a duty."

Born in Austria in 1893, List was the daughter of a baker. Her father forced her into an apprenticeship in a provincial millinery business, considering that her wish to study psychology was an unsuitable way of earning a living. Grudgingly, Adele settled for hatmaking, and worked for several different milliners. After two years in Paris, she returned to open her own millinery business in Vienna's city center in 1926.

List created a very unusual and *avant-garde* shopfront: pure white surrounded by a black frame and with only one hat displayed at a time. Her great interest was religious studies but she had a passion for aesthetics and its historical background. Designing hats was her means of artistic expression as well as providing financial support.

The business grew successfully, employing a *directrice* (manager) and 10 milliners in the workrooms. From 1937 on, Adele List was invited to design two collections a year for Berlin fashion houses, which led to follow-up orders from all over Germany. Never taking her task lightly, Adele was known throughout her life as a great perfectionist and never gave the impression of enjoying her success. However many compliments she received, she was never happy and was forever aiming for greater achievements. Her hat designs were highly artistic, inventive, and crafted to the highest standard. Combining shape, proportion, and texture in a masterly and harmonious way, she created unique pieces of textile sculptures. With an almost religious devotion to her work, List's austere figure looked a little strange in her exquisitely furnished salon, but she had a glamorous and faithful clientele from the world of film and theater. Adele's very special *avant-garde* pieces, however, were never for sale.

She had little time for capricious society ladies, preferring intelligent women with an aim in life. Clients were seen by appointment only, and fittings took place in the evenings,

[Ulrike Koeb, Vienna]

❚ Adele List created soft and feminine hats in the Sixties calling them *Frisur-Turbane* (hairstyle turbans). She liked to use all kinds of materials like straw braids, strips of felt, and pleated, pin-tucked ciré fabric which could blend in with the color of her client's hair

▌This evening hat, created around 1975, was made from felt covered with gold beads and sequins and embroidered by hand. The fringe decoration is detachable and can be worn as a *collier* (elaborate necklace) around the neck

▌Adele List's straw turban designed in 1960 could also be worn back to front, creating a straw wig. List believed that, historically, hair styles and millinery often followed identical trends

so that Adele was never disturbed in her creative work. Finished hats were lovingly wrapped in knotted tissue paper, packed into reinforced boxes, and carried carefully across Vienna to be personally unpacked in the client's home.

List created hats for many fashion shows promoting Viennese style, which was much encouraged and supported by the Nazi rulers, who were resident in Vienna since the *Anschluss* (annexation) in 1938. She loved working with dress designers, who "understood the power and the importance of a hat." For her, Parisian fashion was shallow and frivolous. Adele List's hats were independent creations and never followed any trends or fashion dictates.

In the spring of 1983, the year of her death at age 90, a collection of Adele's hats was assembled for an exhibition by Vienna's University of Applied Art. Many past clients contributed their treasured List hats for the exhibition, which was first shown in Budapest, then toured to Vienna, Berlin, Hamburg, and Paris. In 1993, a new collection of List hats was discovered when Dr. Norbert Zimmer donated 248 List masterpieces to the University of Vienna. The hats had been left by his wife, who had bought many of them, just for the joy and the pleasure of having them, and to preserve them and Adele List's name for posterity.

▌The hair is almost completely tucked away when wearing this plumed cap, which could also be described as a feathered wig. *Picture Post* image 1949

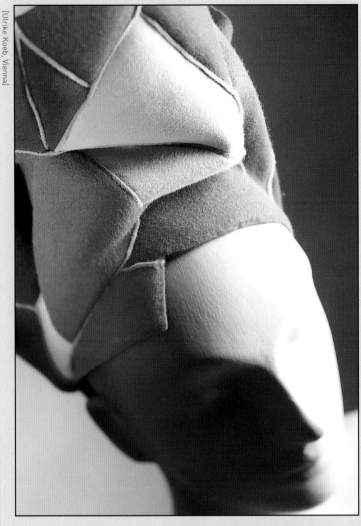

[Ulrike Koeb, Vienna]

[Ulrike Koeb, Vienna]

1990-2000

1980-1990

1970-1980

1960-1970

1950-1960

1940-1950

1930-1940

1920-1930

1910-1920

1900-1910

▌This geometrically-cut felt mosaic hat by Adele List was inspired by the stained glass windows in churches and conveys a look of casually-unstructured elegance

▌This feather toque made from naturally-colored turkey quills could be worn over the forehead or at the back of the head. Small cocktail hats of this kind complemented the neat and elegant fashion of the late 1940s

white velvet gas mask-cum-vanity case for practical but glamorous evening wear.

From across the Atlantic came mouthwatering stories of American fashion as British *Vogue* reported in the spring of 1941: "Big hats, little hats, bonnets, turbans...never was there such variety, such invention. Turbans sprouting flowery topknots, or elaborately spiraled, conch-like, and swagged with pearls. Little crocheted masterpieces, clapped on the back of the head. Great bold piratical felts, sweeping up off the face, and worn with a swagger. Huge **coolie** straws, shaped like a leaf, like a pancake, like a tea-tray, and worn straight." These were dream images for women in Britain, who had to cope with German

bombs, wartime deprivations, and blackouts. Any hat lovers' heart would beat a little faster.

Vogue *Surveys the Hat Situation*

Vogue presented ideas and instructions about making hats at home, encouraging readers to retrim old hats and to look out for hats in "striped shirting and woollen suiting." American *Vogue* made a survey of the hat situation, praising the casual hat which had been "quietly going along all sorts of millinery furores," and recommending that readers "ride the wave of hats-that-fit-the-head," because they had been found convenient by French women in case of

bomb alerts. *Vogue* concluded that "sensibleness had been long in coming" and praised the new, small, casual hats as "stabilizers in the hat wardrobe." Set against these were reports of romantic touches in millinery, with descriptions of "a bouquet of a hat, transplanted from the garden, with sprouting spring flowers and salad green grosgrain ribbons." Phrases like these must have plunged readers into summer reveries and provided relief from the depressing news from the battlefront. In another issue, *Vogue* ordered readers "to lift your spirit and those of all beholders with a frivolous flower disk clapped over the forehead," and it urged the readers to compensate for dressing down by "dressing up your head with a dinner hat."

Christian Dior

A New Look

Dior is a name synonymous with *haute couture*. Just the sound of it instills a feeling of luxury and elegance, loved by women all over the world. As a young man, Christian Dior was told by a clairvoyant that women would bring him luck and wealth. She clearly forgot to add that his name would go down in fashion history.

Before his glorious decade in the limelight, Dior spent years of anonymity, ill health, and poverty, scratching out a living as a fashion illustrator and living in friends' houses. The fairy tale unfolded when, aged 41, Dior happened to be the right man in the right place at the right time, with a feeling for what women really wanted. The rest of the story is legend.

One of five children born to a middle-class family, Dior grew up in Normandy, on the northern coast of France. The family moved to Paris, a buzzing artistic center at the time, something which must have played a part in his future development. Avoiding a career in the diplomatic service, Christian Dior opened an art gallery with a friend. This led to drawing lessons and fashion and millinery designs which he sold to design houses like Agnès, Patou, Schiaparelli, and Molyneux. *Le Figaro*, a leading French national, published some Dior designs in 1936 which attracted the attention of Lucien Lelong, an important figure in Parisian fashion during the war years. He offered Dior a job. At this stage Dior had no idea as to how to cut or assemble a garment, but he had strong visions of crinolines and femininity, etched in his memory from the years of his childhood which was a time when women, like his elegant mother, wore sumptuously frilly dresses.

When the war ended in 1945, Parisian *couture* had to be revived to win back its prewar reputation.

Designers were searching for a fashion shape that would make an impact and proclaim a bright new beginning. By sheer chance, Dior was introduced to Marcel Broussac, a rich industrialist with a chain of cotton mills. These established businesses needed new markets for their products. When Dior, a quiet and nervous man, explained his vision of clothes for women to Broussac, the industrialist must have been touched by the conviction in Dior's eyes. A shrewd businessman, Broussac also reasoned that voluminous skirts and petticoats would need lots of fabric, which would keep his mills in production. A few days later, Boussac offered Dior 10 million francs, a business manager, and premises in the Avenue Montaigne, a prestigious Paris address where *La Maison Dior* still has its headquarters today.

Dior recruited 85 staff from various *couture* houses to help him and unveiled his first collection for spring-summer 1947, calling it "Corolla and Figure of Eight." It was an immediate success. *Harper's Bazaar* reported on the furore the new styles caused and explained why this first collection of long, billowing skirts, small, high waists, and narrow shoulders, which Dior had intended to be simple and conservative was "revolutionary" and immensely chic. The sheer opulence of the collection took everyone's breath away. The publicity was not all positive, and voices of opposition from Britain and the United States were heard protesting about the scandalous waste of fabric, when rationing was still in force in their own countries. The anti-Dior elements organized themselves into a Little Below the Knee Club, and held protests with placards saying "Down with the New Look" and "Burn Monsieur Dior." *Picture Post* added the weight of its opinion by stating that: "We are back to the days when fashion was the prerogative of the leisured wealthy woman, and not the everyday concern of typists or housewives."

Dior's Corolla skirts, which he called "my flowers in bloom" used up to 50 yards of material each and cost between $130 and $400—an absolute fortune at the time. In Britain, clothes rationing coupons were still a fact of life. The British government promised no early end to the restrictions, condemning the French for "rolling in yards of silk" when most women across the English Channel did not even have enough soap to wash with.

All the protests did not stop the New Look, as it had been dubbed by an American journalist. Young girls yearned for luxury and femininity. If this meant a backward step into tightly-corseted waists, falsies in brassieres, and tiptoeing on stiletto heels, so be it. Ingenuity and invention came to the aid of women whose clothes buying was limited by coupons; they turned old blackout curtains, tablecloths, and bedsheets into dresses for their daughters. Some worked out a way of making one dress out of two old ones, or assembling the yardage for a skirt by sewing patchwork pieces together using thread unpicked from other clothes. The hunger for femininity among the young was overwhelming and was helped by the Marshall Plan in 1948, which was a vital investment bringing back prosperity as well as making it easier to obtain nylon stockings from America.

Hats complemented the elegant silhouette and, with matching gloves, added the perfect finishing touches to the New Look. The new shape was the mushroom cloche, worn very straight, accentuating the symmetry of the outfits. Cartwheel brims also looked striking with the wide, ankle length outlines. Dior, who had designed hats himself, valued the contribution that a hat made to an ensemble and always had a busy millinery *atelier* in house. One of his most photographed hats had a brim made totally from feathers assembled like sunrays at right angles to the crown. In contrast, he also designed very small hats, which fitted snugly at the back of the head, and blended in so well with the immaculately tailored look of suits and coats. The house models at Dior always wore little hats with veilings down to chin level. It gave them a very elegant and sophisticated look and protected their makeup when they had to slip dresses over their heads during fashion shows.

Dior's rise was meteoric and his success exceeded all expectations. His personal reign lasted only a decade, but the Maison Dior has continued to flourish under a line of gifted successors from Yves Saint Laurent in 1957 to John Galliano at the end of the twentieth century.

▌**right** Christian Dior's "cocktail suit" made from blue Persian silk and accessorized by a mushroom cloche hat, 1956

▌**opposite** Christian Dior's *couture* designs of 1998 still draw from the master's "New Look" creations with glittering elegance and feminine wide-brimmed hats

Sensuality, Beauty, and Wit at the Movies

Hollywood played a vital role during the 1940s. Films were a popular and important form of entertainment, a relatively inexpensive pleasure that provided a few hours of warmth and escape from the gray depression of wartime. Newsreels were shown before movies and proved to be a powerful medium for mass communication and wartime propaganda. Westerns reached European screens and opened up a dream world of heroism and bravado, while women's films provided emotional drama and longed-for romance.

In the postwar years, 20 million people went to the movies every week. The world-famous Cannes Film Festival was inaugurated in France in 1947, an annual event and meeting point for directors, stars, and would-be starlets. Hollywood stars were revered icons and dream figures and played their part as leaders of fashion and style.

Luton and the English Straw Hat Industry

Straw is a cheap, lightweight material and has been used for hatmaking since antiquity. Many cultures over centuries discovered that straw could be split, woven, plaited, and shaped, and transformed into lightweight headgear as protection against the sun.

Tuscany, in northern Italy, has historically been known for its fine straw hats since the fifteenth century. The finest Florentine straw hats have traditionally been made from the locally grown spring wheat, called *marzelano*, which used to be grown especially for the Florentine hat industry. The straw blades were harvested early in the summer, dried under the Italian sun, bleached by moonlight and finely split and plaited into very thin braids. The narrow plaits were sewn by hand in a spiral shape, until, after about one hundred rows, they formed a finished hat.

A cottage industry of straw plaiters established itself in England during the eighteenth and nineteenth century, and settled around Bedfordshire, north of London. It is thought that refugees from

Straw plaiting in Bedfordshire, England in the early nineteenth century, when 14,000 people earned their living by making straw hats. Children worked long hours in over 100 Plaiting Schools, until this cruel practice was outlawed in 1871

Europe might have imported their skills and they eventually established a thriving straw hat industry that made Luton into the hatting town of the nineteenth and twentieth century. Parts of Bedfordshire were non-conformist and had a reputation of a free-thinking welcoming spirit, which attracted emigrants and new ideas. The local aristocratic family and its Anglican clergy had moved out in the 1820s and made it easy for small businesses to grow without financial or legal restrictions. Hard work was the governor of self-made men and women, who worked on farms and at home, straw plaiting every spare hour of the day. The only recreational time was at the Baptist Chapel, which also served as a social center for newcomers to the area.

The plaits were hand sewn into hats by women in sewing rooms all over the county. One of the seamstresses, Mrs Edward Stratford, adapted a domestic sewing machine for plait sewing in 1873 and increased business in her husband's company, Willcox & Gibbs, the founders of the 10-Guinea Machine which is still in use today

1990-2000

1980-1990

1970-1980

1960-1970

1950-1960

1940-1950

1930-1940

1920-1930

1910-1920

1900-1910

The Plaiting Schools

Straw plaiting dominated home life during the nineteenth century. While the men worked as farm labourers, women and children plaited endless straw braids at home, which were bundled and sold at market in the Plait Hall. To increase the production, Plaiting Schools were established, where children as young as four had to plait up to 17 yards of straw daily, often under cramped, deplorable conditions. In the middle of the nineteenth century there were 102 such schools in the area with 1,457 children, whose only education was listening to readings from the Bible while they plaited endless straw braids, sometimes working up to 14 hours a day. Eventually enlightened members of the clergy became concerned and a test case in 1871 outlawed plaiting schools as an evil, which led to their final closure by the end of the nineteenth century.

The sewing of hats was done by hand, starting with a small button at the top and overlapping one row with another, hand sewing each row with tiny, concealed stitches. It was skilled work and required a long apprenticeship. Communal sewing rooms established themselves in villages, where work was done to order for larger companies. Womenfolk were kept very busy and Luton earned itself the reputation of a place where men were provided for by their working women.

The plaited and sewn hats were blocked, stiffened with gelatin or shellac and trimmed in one of the small factories that had sprouted up in town. Although the practice of hand plaiting came to end at the turn of the century, Luton was still thriving on straw hat manufacturing with imported plaits and hoods from the Far East until about 1920, when felt hat production started and London millinery businesses opened their own factories producing ready-to-wear hat lines.

Engineering and other industries have since taken over in the town of Luton, and hat manufacturing these days takes place on a much smaller scale. The local soccer team is still affectionately known as "The Hatters," and Luton's coat of arms displays a wheatsheaf in memory of all the plaiting fingers which have contributed to the prosperity of the town.

The Beret

FROM THE ARK TO URBAN STREETWEAR

Has there ever been a headgear that goes so far back in history and is as versatile and as expressive as the simple beret, also known as the *béret basque*? This flat, rounded piece of felted cloth, worn tilted forward, backward, or sideways, is strongly associated with the image of a French peasant riding on a bicycle, *Gaulloise* cigarette hanging from his mouth, and a bread baguette under his arm.

It is probably less well-known that the beret dates back to biblical times, because it is said that Noah made the first beret after he saved the animals in his ark. The story goes that when the deluge approached and all living creatures were threatened with drowning, Noah lined his ark with fleece from his sheep to make it more comfortable for his four-footed passengers. The animals trampled on it with wet hoofs during the journey, unwittingly felting it. When the ark came to rest and everybody was safe on dry land, Noah was left with a quantity of felted cloth at the bottom of his ship. He fashioned himself a hat as a useful waterproof protection in the event of another downpour.

Another theory about the origin of this flat woollen hat has been the subject of many debates in the Pyrénées, the mountain chain between France and Spain, known as the Basque country. The question was whether the name *béret basque* was accurate. Had it not been the home-loving Béarnais from the Béarn area across the other side of the mountain, who really invented it?

Whichever account is true, history records shepherds idling summers away by spinning wool and knitting hats with big needles made from twigs. They had learned the craft of knitting from the Arabs who invaded during the eighth century. The Arabs in turn had learned their skills from Egypt, where knitting is shown on ancient tombs. The shepherds soaked the knitted hats in mountain streams and felted them by bashing them on rocks, after which they were dried in the sun, and provided warm, waterproof protection against the snow and the cold of the winter months.

Bérets basques are still manufactured in the southwest of France. Each beret follows the same stages of production as the shepherds' berets, except that the knitters are women using machines and the felting and shaping is done in a factory.

❚ Béarnais shepherds wearing the original *béret basque* in the high Pyrenéan mountains

From Gascogny, the *béret basque* spread north and all over France. The people of Béarn turned their shepherds' felting skills into a prosperous industry, producing not only berets, but also *chéchias* and fezzes for export to the Arab world. As people moved from the land in search of work in towns, the countryfolk took their beloved berets with them, making them symbols of proletarian headgear. Eventually schoolteachers, girls in convent schools, monks, and boy scouts all adopted and came to love the *béret basque*.

The Basques were great adventurers, soldiers, travelers, and fishermen. This may be a reason why the beret appeared in Scotland where it was called the blue bonnet. The shepherd's beret also became military headgear, when it was adopted at the beginning of the century by an elite French Alpine troop, called *Chasseurs Alpins*, who called the beret the *tarte alpine*.

During World War II maroon-colored berets were worn by British airborne troops, and red ones are worn by the Parachute Regiment. The tank corps wore black, commando units had green berets, as well as the United States Marines. The RAF Regiment, meanwhile, wore dark blue ones. Field Marshal Montgomery, Commander-in-Chief of the British forces during World War II, always wore a beret which had been presented to him by the French *Chasseurs Alpins* Regiment after World War I.

Interestingly, the beret was not only a uniform hat of many official military regiments, but it was also adopted by revolutionaries and terrorists. Argentine Che Guevara, wearing a black beret with a star, became an instantly identified image of political struggle and the Cuban Revolution and the fight for freedom generally.

▌Faye Dunaway starring in *Bonnie and Clyde*, playing a woman who seeks excitement in her life by becoming Clyde Barrow's partner in crime. She wears a youthful beret epitomizing Sixties rebelliousness and casual chic

In the 1980s, the Guardian Angels chose to wear bright red berets, when on patrol in the New York subways, the Paris *métro*, or the London Underground. United Nations forces are sometimes referred to as "blueberries" (blue berets) because of their headgear in civilian life, the beret was accepted at the turn of the century as a practical and *avant-garde* headgear by Parisian painters around Montmartre. Artist Pablo Picasso wore a beret and so did writer Ernest Hemingway. Britain's ex-king, the Duke of Windsor, wore a beret when he played golf.

During the 1920s the beret was worn by women who wanted to show how emancipated they were. Coco Chanel designed versions of the *béret basque*, and Greta Garbo was often seen wearing one. Singer Madonna, 1980s female role model, wore a black beret and dark glasses when trying to escape from her sexy image. The beret went brutal in *Bonnie and Clyde*, directed by Arthur Penn in 1967 when Faye Dunaway portrayed a gun-toting female gangster and won an Oscar nomination for her role. Kangol berets, worn back to front, became an accepted symbol of African American cool urban streetwear. Monica Lewinski, the ex-White House intern who embarrassed President Clinton, liked to wear a black DKNY beret. Who knows, maybe in years to come people will argue that chic little hat almost capped his career. And so the stories go on... What would Noah have thought about it all?

The Golden Years

THE FIRST YEARS OF THE SECOND HALF OF THE CENTURY WERE MARKED by a strong sense of recovery and hope for a democratic and prosperous future where war would never come again. World peace, so longed for, was an uneasy one because of fear of communism and the Soviet Union. The Iron Curtain that came down across Central Europe created an economic division and threatened peace again. The world was divided between capitalism and communism, two opposing doctrines that were to fuel political debate and conflicts for decades. Life on either side of the Iron Curtain was not easy during the 1950s, as countries ruined by war rebuilt their economies. The economic revival in Western Europe, helped by American aid under the Marshall Plan, surged ahead. Germany's *Wirtschaftswunder* (economic miracle) years were watched with admiration by other European nations. Optimism filled the air, rationing and shortages came to an end, and slowly people were able to indulge in little luxuries again. *Joie de vivre*—the joy of being alive—was expressed in a flurry of activity, with fresh design ideas and innovation.

Nostalgia in a New Look

Fashion, unlike art and architecture, was moving forward, with one eye on the past and the romantic styles of the *Belle Epoque*. After the gray self-sufficiency of the war years, there was a great hunger for "old-fashioned" femininity and the return to a traditional woman's role of wife and motherhood.

The New Look, a fashion of fragility and beauty, was welcomed by women, who were happy to be victims of their own vanity.

Audrey Hepburn

DO GENTLEMEN PREFER BLONDES?

*H*ollywood satisfied the demand for femininity by producing a line-up of stars whose only role on screen was to be busty, sexy, and blonde. New names were Jayne Mansfield, Diana Dors, and Anita Ekberg, but Marilyn Monroe topped them all with her sex-kitten image in *Gentleman Prefer Blondes* and *How to Marry a Millionaire*. Marilyn—voluptuous, vivacious, and capricious— became the dream woman for men and women, epitomizing the female image of the decade.

The fame of Dutch-born actress Audrey Hepburn during the second half of the1950s could not have been in starker contrast. Her gamine femininity, demure charm, and simple, chic clothes were irresistible and set a new trend for elfin looks and fresh, youthful fashion. She looked exquisite in hats—neat pill-box shapes and deep brimmed hats in many variations. Her most famous style was the Tiffany cloche, a slightly rounded brim, which encased her face down to the eyebrows.

Audrey Hepburn's innocent, girlish image could transform itself instantly into expensive chic and refined luxury. Her delicate beauty and elegance and her ethereal face with her unforgettable eyes could melt icebergs. As Gigi in the Broadway show she was ravishing, charmingly gamine in the movie *Funny Face*, and pure class in *Breakfast at Tiffany's*. Her favorite designer, Hubert de Givenchy, dressed her in eight films and long after her film career had ended. This great man of couture could not have found a more exquisite model and muse.

Audrey Hepburn's own life story "from ugly duckling to glamor lady" repeated itself in many of her films, but in none more pointedly than in *My Fair Lady*, based on George Bernard Shaw's story

Pygmalion. This well-known fairytale-come-true was filmed in 1964 with designs by Cecil Beaton and directed by George Cukor. Audrey Hepburn will always be remembered for the spectacular clothes she wore as Eliza Doolittle, dressed for Royal Ascot with her enormous, extraordinary Ascot hat.

▌ opposite Eliza Doolittle in *My Fair Lady* in a pink silk organza picture hat with frivolous soft frills inspired by styles of the *Belle Epoque*

▌ left Audrey Hepburn in *Breakfast at Tiffany's* unforgettably dressed from head to toe by her favorite designer, Hubert de Givenchy. The hat shape has gone down in millinery history as the "tiffany cloche"

❚ *Vogue's* winner of the model contest June 1952. The elegant New Look outfit, with a soft silk bow, long gloves, parasol, and a flat cloche hat placed on a sleek hairstyle, was the desired fashion image at the time

When the yearning for femininity was satisfied and the New Look began to look dated, a quartet of Parisian *couturiers*—Dior, Balmain, Balenciaga, and Jacques Fath—offered straighter outlines which allowed for easier movement. The clothes had all the hallmarks of *couture*: careful cut and tailoring, meticulously accessorized with hats, shoes, and gloves. The Sack-line, the H-line, and the slender Pillar-line appeared in all the fashion magazines and were slavishly followed by the female population on both sides of the Atlantic. Young French designer Hubert de Givenchy, who was more in tune with the lives of modern women, eased the overstyled fashion with cotton shift dresses, three-quarter-length trousers, and flat pumps. Italian *couture* emerged, with Pucci as one of its first great designers. He proposed colorful resort clothes that showed off bare, suntanned legs and sandals, which would have been virtually unheard of a few years earlier.

American designers held their own against the strong French influences which had again monopolized design and *couture* as talented and temperamental New York *couturier* Charles James designed high-class fashion with lush, highly constructed evening gowns. Mainbocher and Hattie Carnegie were established names, and Claire McCardell led the trend for future American fashion with shirtwaister dresses and mix-and-match casual sportswear in denim and cotton.

Hats and Gloves for a Lady-like Look

At the beginning of the decade, hats were still a must for women wishing to achieve a perfectly groomed look. Female employees at British *Vogue* would receive notes reprimanding them if they were seen in their lunch hour without a hat and gloves. By the end of the 1950s, things had changed. Hats no longer dominated the look of an outfit, but had to complement and embellish it. Other accessories—shoes, handbags, and umbrellas—all rivaled the privileged position of hats. Makeup became more obvious with thick, painted eyeliners, charcoal brushed eyebrows, and strongly defined red lips. Hairdressers became more affordable and

The coming-out season—when marriageable young women from high society were presented at court in the hopes of finding a husband—was revived in London. Fashion magazines were full of beauty advice, and the increasing production of goods for the mass market made fashion accessible to a wider circle of women than ever before.

Young women in bouncy, flowery dresses with three-layered petticoats transformed the streets of postwar Europe and North America. Inexpensive chainstores like Macy's in New York, Prisunic in Paris, and Marks and Spencer in London responded to the appetite for postwar consumerism with wide selections of the latest styles. New shops,

called boutiques, sprang up in suburbs and country towns, offering chic mix-and-match clothes and accessories.

Parisian *couture* flourished, benefiting not only from rich private clients but also from foreign buyers in a thriving ready-to-wear industry. Many European Jewish refugees, who had settled in Britain and the United States, brought their expertise to this sector of the fashion business. Peace and prosperity are fundamentals for a fashion industry, which reached new heights of elegance in the 1950s. The mood was for dressing up, before the youth culture of the 1960s and 1970s dictated "dressing down" as the dominant fashion theme.

New Look hats were created in many different shapes; a wavy seashell cloche framing the face reminiscent of the demure bonnet of the past

1990–2000

1980–1990

1970–1980

1960–1970

1950–1960

1940–1950

1930–1940

1920–1930

1910–1920

1900–1910

Paulette

THE QUEEN OF THE TURBAN

Parisian milliners were still dominant either in specialized businesses or working under the name of a famous *couture* house. Maud Roser was millinery designer at Dior, Svend worked for Jacques Fath, and Balmain had his own *atelier* showing youthful straw **capelines** in his collections. New names appeared: Gilbert Orcel, who designed beautiful flower hats, Emme, Vernier, and the young Jean Barthet, as well as Simone Mirman who moved her business to London and became one of the milliners who styled hats for the Queen.

But the greatest name, and undisputed star of hat design in the 1950s and beyond was Paulette. Last in a line of *grandes modistes*, Paulette was a formidable personality as well as a very beautiful woman, who had started her fashion career as a model. She simply loved hats, looked exquisite wearing them, and had the artistic flair and taste needed for the creation of irresistible designs. Having no training in hatmaking herself, she employed a milliner called Monette to provide the technical know-how that Paulette lacked. Together they set about building a very successful business.

As it was fashionable in *couture* circles to put the diminutive *ette* at the end of girls' names, Paulette and Monette took on Josette, a young apprentice who stayed with them for 30 years and still runs a hat salon in Paris, in keeping with the spirit of her teacher and mentor, Paulette. La Maison Paulette on Avenue Franklin D. Roosevelt had a worldwide reputation serving the rich and famous and employed 125 milliners and eight *vendeuses*, including two royal princesses, known as *vendeuses mondaines*, who worked for fun and only on commission, acting as a link with the aristocratic clientele.

At the twice-yearly collections, up to 120 model hats were unveiled at the salon; it was a social event not to be missed. During one show, Paulette sent the fashion models out on the catwalk with suitcases containing six different foldable hats, which the models pulled on their heads one by one. She had invented the **chapeau mou**, a delightful soft turban of great sophistication that no elegant lady of the 1950s could be without.

[Illustration by Fiona Tromans, 1991]

Paulette's famous turbans were soft and practical but also stylish and chic. A turban covered and protected hairstyles and was an essential fashion item for Parisian women

Paulette's passion for the turban started when she wrapped a piece of fabric around her head when she cycled around Paris during the war, but she refined her skills so that no other milliner could drape jersey or silk like her, guiding the fabric with her fingers into flattering folds and shapes. The secret of Paulette's more sophisticated turbans has its source on the glorious day that Paris was liberated in June 1944. French troops paraded down the Champs-Elysées, to the tune of the French national anthem and *tricolore* flags waving everywhere. All of Paris turned out to watch, including Madame Paulette. When she saw a French colonial regiment with Algerian soldiers marching along wearing turbans, she got quite excited, pulled a soldier to one side, insisting that he tell her the secret of his turban. Rushing back to the salon, Paulette grabbed a *poupée* (canvas dummy) and pinned a large box of matches on it as a foundation shape. She then began to drape a piece of fabric, just as the Algerian soldier had told her. The famous and inimitable Paulette turban was born, becoming her trademark classic and featured at the end of every collection.

As wearing hats became less popular in the 1960s and 1970s, Paulette's business shrank but her fame as one of the best postwar milliners never died. She worked closely with Otto Lucas in London, who produced Paulette hats under license in London and New York. Paulette never retired from her studio and created hats right up to her death on September 9, 1984.

❚ Paulette's inimitable sense of style and beauty made her hats collectors' pieces for women all over the world

London Collections

Paris—first report

Signs of Spring in the shops

MARCH 1951 · PRICE 3/6
THE CONDÉ NAST PUBLICATIONS LTD.

Vogue cover 1951 shows a plain pillbox hat, open at the back to complement the low chignon, a nostalgic hairstyle of the turn of the century

viscose led to the development of cellophane, which opened up more possibilities in the design of braids like fine pedaline and neoraband, giving milliners interesting new materials to work with. Horsehair fiber was replaced by a semi-synthetic material which came to be known as **crinoline** and added transparency to straw braids and trimmings. The variety of natural and artificial straw braids was infinite and provided a splendid choice of novelties for every season.

Bibis: Frivolous Hats forAfter Dark

An important new trend in millinery was the evening hat, worn to the theater or out to dinner. Evening hats could be anything from stiff disk brims sitting straight above the eyebrows to little caps snugly covering the back of the head. Some were clusters of feathers, or beautifully styled large bows nestling in bouffant hairstyles.

The making of these little works of art, called *bibis*, required excellent manual dexterity and millinery skills. Many designs needed sparterie foundations, which had to be shaped and wired before being covered with velvet, satin, or taffeta, and topped with embroidery or beading. A little evening hat could take days to make, requiring the *doigts fins* (agile fingers) of an experienced hatmaker. These highly skilled ladies knew their worth and superiority and were always called *filles* (girls) in a workroom, even if they were over 80 years old.

Cheaper ready-to-wear hats were available in the stores, but factories could never produce a real model hat with its finesse and perfect craftsmanship. This often left a woman with the choice of buying an expensive hat or none at all. Exclusive hats of high quality could never be produced at a reasonable price. The result was that model hats remained a luxury item in a world of increasing mass production and slowly priced themselves out of the market.

Royal Ascot: Where Hats and Horses Meet

The Royal Ascot race meeting is the most glamorous date in the horseracing year. Held

were no longer the privilege of a few. Versatile and inventive hairstyles were created, taking over the role traditionally played by millinery in boosting a woman's confidence.

Hats were not changed several times a day anymore, as during the prewar years, but the styles worn were dramatic and not easy to ignore. The lady-like look demanded spectacular picture hats with low crowns, worn on the back of the head, and framing the face, as bonnets had done in the previous century. Hats had to be rigidly constructed to keep their perfectly symmetrical shapes, and were often made in fabrics which had to be supported by solid materials and wires. Some large brims were wider and sloped at the

sides creating a look almost like a Catholic nun's headdress. There were mushroom brims in braided straw, rounded coolie brims, and Dior's sou'wester, a rounded cloche worn deep into the face. Another shape was the breton, which framed the face and achieved the demure "halo look." Half-bretons turned up at the front and were cut very short at the back.

Straw braids as well as woven exotic straw hoods of the finest quality imported from Switzerland, Italy, and the Far East provided an infinite variety of colors, textures, and designs. Adding to the established Italian natural straws came synthetic cellophane straw from Switzerland. The invention of

at the British Queen's own racecourse, it takes place every year in the middle of June. The four days are much more about royalty, corporate entertaining, and displaying extravagant hats than about horses. Ascot is the highlight of the English season which starts with horseracing at the Derby in May, goes on to Ascot and rowing at the Henley Royal Regatta in June, to more racing again at "glorious" Goodwood in August, with possibly the tennis tournament at Wimbledon or yachting races of Cowes Week fitted in between. Each of the events, usually patronized by at least one member of the Royal Family, has a sporting activity as a backdrop, but participating and "being seen" means much more than being a sports enthusiast and has deeper, complex social and commercial connotations. Dressing appropriately for each occasion means understanding a complicated, secret code, and wearing the right hat can be the pass port to social acceptance.

Royal Ascot is definitely the most publicized of the summer gatherings which make up the English season. Like all the other events, it offers an opportunity to dress up, see the rich and famous and enjoy lavish hospitality. The tradition of Royal Ascot is an ancient one and dates from 1711, when the first royal race meeting was held by Queen Anne. She opened the day by driving into the racecourse in an open carriage, just as the Royal Family still does today.

Men are required to wear a smart morning suit and an elegant gray top hat, as well as a wallet fat with betting money. After all, it's a sporting event.

For women, the most important and enjoyable of all the planning is deciding on the right Ascot hat. A popular way to start is by planning the hat and finding an outfit to accompany it later. It might be a lavish Eliza Doolittle hat with a wide brim and flowery decorations; perhaps a supremely sleek, elegant number in black and white, or a surreal fun hat, full of imagination and fantasy. The chance to wear something really extraordinary only comes once a year.

One of the particular excitements, awaited by the press and the public alike, is the annual appearance of Mrs Shilling and the betting on what kind of extraordinary hat

▌ *top* During almost three hundred years of history, the annual Royal Ascot horse racing event in June has been a highlight of the British social calendar. This picture was taken at Royal Ascot in 1933

▌ *below* Royal Ascot—as well known for its hats as its horses. Not all are sheer fantasy; some hats are functional like these "periscope hats" designed for superb viewing

she will wear this year. This is a tradition which this extrovert lady adores. Her son, David Shilling, a famous hat designer, creates an Ascot hat for her every year and the Shilling Ascot hats are always extraordinary and witty. One memorable year, there was a 4-foot giraffe hat. Another year David recalls making a top hat, over 3 feet high with a rabbit on top. The 1994 hat was especially ingenious; a sunflower with a tiny bird that sang whenever Mrs Shilling moved and went

quiet when she stopped talking to people.

The most memorable occasion of all was in 1982, just after the Falklands War ended, when David Shilling sat up all night and made a victory hat, patriotically colored red, white, and blue, and edged with white doves of peace. As always, the hat caused a sensation when his mother walked into the royal enclosure, but David remembers and cherishes the approving smile of the Queen, thanking him for this touchingly patriotic gesture.

1990-2000
1980-1990
1970-1980
1960-1970
1950-1960
1940-1950
1930-1940
1920-1930
1910-1920
1900-1910

Aage Thaarup

A Dane Turns Heads in London

People take to making hats in different ways and for different reasons. Danish-born Aage Thaarup fell in love with hats while dusting them in Berlin. In 1926 as a young apprentice in Denmark, he had made contact with an English hat company by peeling postage stamps off hat boxes and sending them to the boss of the company, who was a stamp collector.

Hat dusting took Aage from Berlin to Paris and on to London, where he worked for a small wholesale company, advancing in his career by arranging and packing hats as well as dusting them. Having handled thousands of hats, Aage's dream was to design some. With few savings, he bought some stock and materials from his old contacts in Berlin and a first-class boat ticket to India. He started his business by selling hats on board the ship, making valuable contacts with society ladies as well as raising money for the sailors' benevolent fund. On arrival in Bombay, he sold hats to Lady Sykes, wife of the Governor of India. This encouraged him to hire two Indian tailors, who sat cross-legged on the floor and stitched hats under his supervision.

Aage Thaarup never learned to sew, and never held a needle in his hand throughout his career. He could shape hats and knew what he wanted, but most of all he had the gift of charm and vision and could make any woman feel good, cherished, and more beautiful by wearing one of his hats. Returning to London in 1932, he set up a small millinery salon in three rooms on the top floor of a building in Berkeley Square. Hats made with the help of a millinery girl were taken around to be sold in shops all over the city. Aage wrote to Cecil Beaton, who was taking photographs of all the beautiful ladies in London, offering him hats. The breakthrough came when Aage was asked to make a versatile hat for Beaton's youngest sister who was going to Ascot on all four consecutive days of horseracing. "I thought of a large floppy green straw," he remembers in his autobiography. "For the first day I put a little apple twig with a green leaf on it; for the second day apple-blossoms; for the third day a little apple; and for the last day just a little worm. This was the kind of charming nonsense that appealed to Aage.

Loved and accepted by London society, Aage Thaarup made hats for Hollywood actresses, society ladies, the aristocracy, and, most proudly, for the Royal Family. Among the list of illustrious clients were Marlene Dietrich and Margot Fonteyn. He was friends with Salvador Dali, fashion designer Elsa Schiaparelli, and British playwright Terence Rattigan. The Duchess of York came to Berkeley Square for her hats and when she became Queen after Edward VIII abdicated, Aage was summoned to Buckingham Palace and arrived there on his rickety illegal bicycle. Aage also delivered hats for the young princesses and designed Princess Elizabeth's going-away hat after her wedding to the Duke of Edinburgh on November 20, 1947.

Aage Thaarup's unique understanding of women and hats is summed up in his book *Heads and Tales*, which contains memories of some of his favorite designs over the years: "The silly hats, the lovely hats, the important hats, the wicked hats. Hats that made history. Hats that bloomed in high places in the world's capitals. Hats created to blush almost unseen in faraway deserts. Hats that circled the world in aeroplanes, that charmed the world on celluloid. Hats that won sweethearts. Hats that broke hearts, and hats that restored married happiness. Hats that got plain women jobs, and beautiful women into peerage." He created them and loved them all.

Thaarup's theory of millinery was that a hat must be "a creation of realities and dreams" and that it should be remembered with pleasure by those who see it

The Straw Boater

A Very English Hat

Summer days, sunshine, and punting on the river—this quintessentially English picture—would not be complete without young gentlemen attired in straw boaters, the proper headgear of the oarsman.

The ancestor of the boater is almost certainly the sailor's hat, which was issued to midshipmen by the Royal Navy in the latter part of the nineteenth century. Cool and protective from the sun, this straw hat was softer and floppier than the boater, with a small rigid brim and flat crown with a striped silk ribbon trimming.

Boaters were popular summer hats for the middle classes in the early part of the century, and relieved gentlemen from the bowlers worn during the winter months. Straw hats were also fashionable among young gentlemen in the 1920s, who wore them for sports like croquet on manicured, green English lawns. To this day, Cambridge University students enjoy boating on the River Cam, where they have fun punting, with beer and good company.

Around 1900, flat straw hats were popular amongst working-class women in the East End of London. Costers' wives and daughters loved to wear slightly dilapidated boaters made from chip straw and enjoyed decorating them on Sundays with velvet ribbons or garishly-dyed ostrich feathers. If they could not afford real feathers, they made colored paper replicas and other decorations from odd bits of fabric. They would remove the stylish, colorful trimmings during the week, when the hat was decorated modestly, with a plain ribbon.

Sailor hats were worn by young children in Victorian times and straw hats became part of the standard uniform in many private schools in Britain. Trimmed with ribbons of the school's colors, it was obligatory for pupils to wear the hats on special occasions like the annual sports and speech days. Straw boaters as part of a school uniform have diminished since the 1960s, but some established English private schools like Harrow still keep up the tradition.

Maurice Chevalier, the charming French actor and *chansonier* of the Twenties and Thirties will always be remembered by his *canotier*, the French name for a boater. Rarely without his hat, he wore it slightly over one eye, sang and danced with it, and Chevalier's image of a gallant irresistible French *charmeur* was enhanced by the boater which became his trademark.

Today straw boaters are a rare sight except for one annual occasion during the English summer season, the day of Henley Royal Regatta. This is the day when gentlemen, normally attired in gray city suits, don cream flannel trousers, boldly striped blazers, and wear either a schoolboy's rowing cap or a straw boater. It is a very English hat for a very English occasion.

above Auguste Renoir's
Dance at Moulin de la Galette
(1876) when boaters, toppers,
or bowlers were worn by
gentlemen dancing on a
summer evening in Paris

far left Outside Dunn & Co.,
gentleman's outfitters in
London, the hatmakers
parade with piles of popular
straw boaters, circa 1925

left Maurice Chevalier's
straw boater was as much
his trademark as was his
seductive voice. His fans
loved and expected both,
on stage and on screen

1960 – 1970

Youth, Hope, and Music

THE 1960s WAS THE DECADE WHEN JOHN F. KENNEDY WAS ELECTED President of the United States. He was the first president to be born in the twentieth century; the first to hold a press conference on television; and the first not to wear a hat on the day of his inauguration. Kennedy believed in informality, liberalism, democracy, and youth. His election in 1961 was the dawn of a new era of hope for many nations around the world.

In the three short years of Kennedy's presidency astronauts explored outer space. Russian cosmonaut Yuri Gagarin was the first to orbit the earth in 1961, followed by American John Glenn, who circled the earth three times, a year later. In 1969, Neil Armstrong was the first man to walk on the moon, an event Kennedy had predicted in a speech to Congress just after his election in 1961.

Kennedy confronted the Soviet Union during the Cuban missile crisis, but negotiations with Nikita Khrushchev pulled the world back from the brink of nuclear war. Visiting the besieged city of West Berlin in 1962, Kennedy made a rousing speech in the shadow of the Berlin Wall. He believed in equal opportunity for all and defended Martin Luther King, Jr. during the 1963 civil rights campaign. John F. Kennedy was assassinated in Dallas, Texas, on November 22, 1963, a moment in history, and ingrained in the memory of everyone who was alive on that fateful day.

The Swinging Sixties

The Swinging Sixties followed a decade which had brought prosperity to the Western world. Young people had grown up in

Otto Lucas

A VISION FOR HATS

Otto Lucas remains an unforgettable name in the hat world. He built up an extremely successful wholesale millinery business, which made him a millionaire.

He was not a trained milliner, nor was he a designer, but he had taste and vision. He knew what he could sell and he surrounded himself with talented and competent people, who contributed to the phenomenal success of his business. Designers brought over from France created hat collections under Otto's beady eye, the sales director charmed hat buyers, and the vast workroom produced the orders to be sent around the world.

German by birth, Otto arrived in London as an agent for an Austrian hat company and had set up his business in 1937. World War II forced him into four years of internment, but his company continued and flourished after his release, to become the top wholesale millinery company in London. Ruling his empire with a iron fist, Otto Lucas regularly reduced some of the people around him to tears. He plunged *vendeuses* in the top Parisian *couture* houses into a state of panic, whenever he decided, on the spur of the moment, to fly over to Paris to buy wonderful hats and also to stock up on bundles of fresh asparagus, his favorite vegetable.

Otto Lucas had nothing in common with the street fashion of Biba or Mary Quant except for his firm belief that whatever Paris did, London could do better. He made his salon in London's Bond Street the center of the best millinery design in the world. During the 1950s and 1960s the powerful American stores used to send their buyers to Paris to view the new collections, totally ignoring what London had to offer. In a dramatic gesture, Lucas chartered a plane and flew Marge Browning, the most respected American buyer, to London to show her his newest hats. She was captivated, and paved the way for his business in New York, telling *Vogue* to always check with Otto Lucas for new trends in fashion.

Otto Lucas sold quantities of his ready-to-wear styles, as well as model hats, to the prestigious New York stores and Philip Somerville, who used to accompany Otto Lucas on his selling trips,

[Henry Clarke] © Vogue/Condé Nast Publications Ltd

▌ Otto Lucas's unique eye for style was acclaimed on both sides of the Atlantic. A small turned-up brim in silk with stitched flower petal decoration for *Vogue* February 1961

▌Elegance with a plain city suit and romantic silk flower beret for
Vogue February 1961

▌Elegance, sophistication, and flattering wearability was Lucas's
trademark shown in this off-the-face, machine-stitched model
in soft gray silk

remembers the glamor of these occasions. Buyers were taken out to the best restaurants and treated to private hat shows, which took place in the seventh-floor Plaza Hotel suite that Lucas always occupied on his visits to New York. Specially hired American models paraded the hats and would either be applauded or dismissed with cries of: "Oh, it's a pot, just take it away!"—the signal for Philip Somerville to make sure that the hat disappeared swiftly into its box.

Feared by many and highly respected by others, Otto could make or break people and did not suffer fools gladly. He demanded total devotion from his workforce and directed his designers like a powerful opera conductor would urge his musicians. In 1937 when he hired Miss Jolly, who later became his confidante and business manager, she was told firmly not to wear anything but black, set off with a single row of pearls around her neck. She kept to the rule for years until, after Lucas's funeral in 1972, she went out and bought herself, with great delight, a bright red dress.

Around this time in millinery, there seemed to be a kind of reversal of roles. Where women had tended to dominate hat design, many men now came to the fore. Aage Thaarup, the Queen's milliner, was later followed by his pupil, John Boyd, who set up his own salon in 1946. The young Graham Smith had returned from Paris, where he had designed for Lanvin, and Frederick Fox had arrived from Australia and was working with Hardy Amies, one of the Queen's dress designers.

Exciting newcomer James Wedge embraced young Sixties fashion with hats for his swinging King's Road shops, Top Gear and Countdown. The Wedge leather cap that John Lennon wore has gone down in photo history along with "baby bonnets" for skinny Sixties teenagers in flat sandals. A versatile hatter, he had a strong interest in clothes and fashion photography. One story tells that Wedge bought Westminster Abbey chorister's smocks and sold them the same afternoon as minidresses in his King's Road shop.

Manhattan's
Mr John

NEW YORK'S PRIDE

John Pico John, known as Mr John, was the top milliner during the 1950s and 1960s and his salon was *the* place in New York for chic ladies to buy hats. Mr John had been in a very successful partnership with milliner Frederic Hirst since 1928, under the label John-Frederics, and had set up his own business in Manhattan in 1948.

Mr John had arrived from Germany as a child, and learned how to make hats from his mother. Embarrassed that his German name Harberger was being mispronounced as "Hamburger," he dropped it and became Mr John. His widespread reputation for beautiful hats made society women—among them the Duchess of Windsor, Lauren Bacall, and Joan Crawford—flock to his illustrious salon.

Mr John's proudest achievement was making the hats for Vivien Leigh in *Gone with the Wind*. He loved working for films, and also created Marilyn Monroe's hats in *Gentleman Prefer Blondes*, as well as Marlene Dietrich's in *Shanghai Express*. British society photographer and set designer Cecil Beaton consulted Mr John on the design of his black and white extravaganza for *My Fair Lady*, which must have been one of the most spectacular hats in millinery history.

Sadly, Mr John's business declined during the 1970s, which he blamed on "the Sixties orthopedic hairdos and fresh fried curls," as he described the new hairstyles. He made hats for some of his loyal private clients until just before he died at the age of 91.

right Audrey Hepburn, photographed by Cecil Beaton, in a striking hat by Mr John adding an element of asymmetry to an otherwise symmetrical image

Princess Grace of Monaco, the former American film star Grace Kelly, in a soft turban decorated with silk flower petals

the years of plenty, but many started to question the complacent materialism of the postwar period. The younger generation, as always, rejected the established values of their parents and searched for an unconventional lifestyle and freedom of expression. Most of all, they denounced the dictatorship of Parisian fashion designers, which their mothers followed slavishly. Teenagers could not see the relevance of expensive couture to their new lifestyles. Many were financially independent and wanted to spend their money on records, make-up, cigarettes, hairstyles, and inexpensive clothes. Novelty was more important than quality for the 1960s "drop-out" generation. They shocked their parents and society with long hair, listening to outrageous pop groups like the Beatles, and raising the hemlines of dresses to way above the knee. The miniskirt was born.

London was taking over the fashion lead from Paris. For the first time in fashion history, new styles were created in the streets and not in secretive haute couture houses in Paris. British designer Mary Quant opened her first shop, Quant's Bazaar, in London's

King's Road in 1955, causing a sensation with customers queuing up outside, desperate to try on the "gear," as the new inexpensive ranges of clothes were called. Within seven years, Mary Quant was an established designer with a multi-million-dollar business, producing lines of clothes and make-up, and supplying 150 shops in the UK and 320 in America.

Biba, another Sixties phenomenon in London, became almost a lifestyle for its followers. The first shop in Kensington Church Street was created by Barbara Hulanicki and expanded into the Biba "emporium" in nearby Kensington High Street, becoming a shrine of worship for teenagers from all over Europe. With its exotic decor Biba provided a total look: clothes, accessories, and glittering make-up in shiny, black containers.

The new wave of designers in the early 1960s wanted to erase established fashion and create a fashion democracy of street styles. Just like the new music by the Beatles and the Rolling Stones, they swept away old rules, only to find themselves imposing new ones. The great romantic vision was a victim of its own success, and commercialism began to erode some of the brave, rebellious ideas. Young women of this decade might not have wanted to have fashion dictated, but they were happy to be led.

Sixties fashion phenomenon was model Twiggy, an extremely thin, childlike waif, with big baby eyes, pigtails, and fake freckles painted on her nose. The aim was to look like an awkward 14-year-old teenager. Sophistication was seen as outdated by the new generation, and elegant hats were not part of this young fashion image. Fashionable beehive hairstyles did not accommodate hats easily either but perhaps the most negative aspect for millinery was that expensive model hats were seen as an immoral luxury.

Many millinery businesses had to reduce their workforces and some closed down, taking with them many of the specialized affiliated trades such as the feather- and flowermakers. Wholesale millinery businesses which had developed a quality ready-to-wear range survived and captured the remaining market. Not all women wanted to look like little urchins, and elegance and

quality was still accepted as *de rigueur*, the right thing to wear, by the older generation.

Men in Design

Male millinery designers took over the reign during the 1960s and Paris was no exception with notable names like Gilbert Orcel, Jacques Pinturier, Jean-Charles Brosseau, and, most famous of them all, Jean Barthet. Barthet was a full-blooded, charismatic man with all the warmth and charm of his native Midi, in the South of France. He opened his business in Paris in 1949 and was adored by his clientele, which included Princess Grace of Monaco, and actresses Sophia Loren, Brigitte Bardot, and Catherine Deneuve.

Barthet's hats combined traditional elegant millinery with Sixties informality and style. The personality of his clients was what mattered most to him, and many women fell in love with his flattering and imaginative styles. He was much admired by the wholesale buyers from Britain and the United States, who knew and appreciated his instinctive sense of shape and proportion. Jean Barthet hats had a special combination of femininity and a clean modern line, and were always the most flattering and desirable of millinery creations.

The Secrets of La Maison Michel

During the 1950s and 1960s, exchanges in the millinery world between London, New York, and Paris had one vital contact point in the Rue Ste-Anne, in Paris. Tucked away at the back of a charming courtyard, and known only to insiders in the millinery world, is La Maison Michel. The front door may look like an ordinary Parisian apartment block entrance, but when it opens there is no mistaking the heady perfume of a millinery *atelier*—an accumulation over decades of the smells of stiffening, steaming, and blocking the millions of hats which have passed through this Mecca of the millinery world.

La Maison Michel was founded in 1936 by Monsieur Heusser, a Swiss millinery agent who wanted to centralize the activities of a diffused hat industry. He imported felts and straws in large quantities and offered a blocking service to smaller businesses, as

1990–2000
1980–1990
1970–1980
1960–1970
1950–1960
1940–1950
1930–1940
1920–1930
1910–1920
1900–1910

A flamingo velvet pillbox hat with a pleated front and bow, from the Autumn collection by Christian Dior Chapeaux Ltd. 1961

▌Sophia Loren—glamorous Sixties film star, sophisticated society lady, and fashion icon—in a black brimmed felt hat with fine veiling

▌London's Swinging Sixties were reflected in music, dance, and a boom in street fashion, propelled by the technical advances in clothing

well as a valuable source of supply of materials. La Maison Michel also made hats to order for *couture* houses which did not have their own millinery *ateliers*. Providing a link for the industry, it was the first port of call for foreign buyers, who were directed to the appropriate designers and collections. La Maison Michel could, and still does, supply foreign buyers with hat designs, the wooden blocks needed for production, and the materials for making up the orders. Felt and straw can be dyed to the tones required by an associated company on the floor below. Michel provides a total service, with a little bit of the latest gossip thrown in.

From the Sixties to the Eighties, Pierre Debard ran this very successful business. The workrooms are supervised by his attractive wife, Claudine, herself a first-class milliner, who feels that she is the "last link in the chain of *couture* milliners in Paris." Pierre remembers his biggest clients, Otto Lucas from London and Lilly Daché from New York, who used to buy 50 model hats, with matching sparterie shapes. They ordered wooden blocks for each hat, and quantities of straws, felts, and fabrics. All this had to be assembled very quickly, packed, and shipped abroad to be copied and produced in Britain and the United States. "That was big business." says Pierre, with the memory glowing in his eyes, "Those days will never come back again!"

Even lean years for millinery in the 1970s were busy *chez* Michel. Pierre remembers the craze for larger and larger hats led by designers like Christian Lacroix. The only way to make these large brims was in *paille cousue* (sewn straw braid), and La Maison Michel was the only *atelier* that could supply the materials and produce the hats. Downstairs in the blocking room is the evidence of these cartwheel hats with wooden blocks of over three feet in diameter, needing two people to lift them.

Patrice Wolfer, the current managing director at La Maison Michel, took over from Pierre 11 years ago. He, too, was lured by the heady perfume of millinery, which brought back childhood memories. Passionate about hats and beautiful fabrics, he presides over rooms and cupboards full of exquisite, old stock with a mixture of pride and despair.

1990–2000
1980–1990
1970–1980
1960–1970
1950–1960
1940–1950
1930–1940
1920–1930
1910–1920
1900–1910

Jackie Kennedy

FIRST LADY'S STYLISH PILLBOX

Millinery history was also created by the all-American designer Halston, known simply as "H" to his numerous friends, including Liza Minelli and Andy Warhol in the 1960s, as well as Bianca Jagger and Marisa Berenson in the 1980s.

The name which will always be linked to his designs is Jackie Kennedy, for whom he created the unforgettable **pillbox** hat in 1961. Roy Halston Frowick, to give him his full name, had learned millinery with Lilly Daché and joined Bergdorf Goodman New York in 1958 working with the brilliant Jessica Daube, who was largely responsible for the department store's reputation in millinery. He expanded into dress design and became a much loved jet-setter, as well as one of the best American designers of the 1970s, always representing simplicity and purity of style.

The story of the Jackie Kennedy pillbox started when the future First Lady was looking for a hat to wear to her husband's presidential inauguration. Halston decided with Jackie to make her a plain pillbox hat which suited her dress style. The simple but stylish hat caused a fashion sensation across the Western world, when many people watched the inauguration ceremony on television, one cold day in January, 1961. The dent that Jackie accidentally put in the hat as she climbed out of the presidential limousine was interpreted as a special design feature, and the dented pillbox hat was immediately copied around the world. The pillbox became Jackie Kennedy's personal trademark, and she wore the same hat style in fabrics or colors to match her outfits. The final one, the pink pillbox which she wore during the fatal drive through the streets of Dallas, was splattered with blood as her husband lay dying in her arms.

❙ Jackie Kennedy favored small hats worn to the back of her head. It was new and youthful look, loved by the media as it allowed her face to be photographed from all angles

One story about Jackie which is less well known is that she used a milliner at Bergdorf Goodman as an adviser for her meticulously planned wardrobe. Documented in 13 letters to Marita O'Connor, the First Lady makes detailed suggestions and even sketches of hats she wanted Marita to make for her. In one letter, Jackie asks if Marita could act as her personal shopper at Bergdorf Goodman, an idea which was way ahead of its time. In one of the final letters, written in 1966, Jackie requests a hat as a disguise to help protect her privacy. The then former First Lady wrote: "Could you please make me a hat as a private New Yorker rather than a First Lady— perhaps a beret, the ordinary kind children have. I just can't find one big enough. I want to wear it in the park when it's raining."

Catherine Deneuve

HATS AND DARK GLASSES

After a series of voluptuous, sexy movie stars like Marilyn Monroe from the USA, Brigitte Bardot from France, and Gina Lollobrigida from Italy, the serious, elegant beauty of French actress Catherine Deneuve was like a cool drink after too much chocolate. Deneuve's pure and eternal beauty conveyed the image of a grown-up woman, as an antidote to the Twiggy girlishness of the early 1960s. Her performance in *Belle de Jour*, a 1967 film by Luis Bunuel, where she plays a prostitute by day and a frigid, suburban housewife by night, was a masterpiece of ambiguity and ice-cool sophistication. Her wardrobe for the film was designed by French *couture* designer Yves Saint Laurent, and between them they launched the "hat with dark glasses look"—a curious blend of anonymity and instant recognition at the same time.

Deneuve's beauty was made for the Saint Laurent look, or perhaps it is the other way round. The encounter with Catherine Deneuve was as significant for the young French designer as the one with Pierre Bergé at Christian Dior's funeral, which was the start of a lifelong association, on which the Saint Laurent empire was built. Yves Saint Laurent had been assistant to Dior and had absorbed the ethos of traditional *haute couture*, but he also understood that women wanted to free themselves from slavishly following fashion. Embracing the change in women's lifestyles and the mood of the times, his genius lay in combining the two seemingly opposing doctrines of *couture* and modern life. He understood that the clock of fashion evolution would never be turned back.

❚ Romantic sophistication portrayed by Deneuve in a large straw hat designed by Barthet, one of the last great milliners from Paris

Brigitte Bardot in Jean Barthet's floppy-brimmed flowerpot cloche with gingham headscarf tied, bonnet-style, under the chin

rare for any woman in those days. What was even more daring and unusual was that she started to preach Christianity to the people around her. She had a vision of the Virgin Mary and Jesus, who gave her a ring as a sign of an eternal bond. From that day, Catherine believed herself engaged to Christ and refused all other propositions of marriage, to the great despair of her family and parents. She became a martyr for her faith and later the saint to whom all unmarried women over 25 prayed when they wanted to escape from parental pressure to marry.

Centuries after these dramatic events in Sinai, where Saint Catherine lies buried in a beautiful Byzantine monastery, her feast day is celebrated as a holiday for all *couture ateliers* in Paris. An occasion for dressing up, with lots of eating and drinking, it usually ends with a ball in the evening. The *Catherinettes* (all young women over 25 and unmarried) are dressed in elaborate green and yellow costumes, which have been lovingly prepared by their workroom colleagues. The hats take center stage, as extravagant creations, again in bright yellow and green to signify the colors of fertility and hope. The youngest members in the workroom usually prepare a play in costumes with the management of the *couture* houses as guests of honor. It is a great opportunity to have a party, create fantastic hats and costumes, dress up, dance, have fun, and maybe even find a husband at the ball.

Expanding on his contradictory feelings, Wolfer explains: "I love hats, creating them, making them, and bringing them to life," however he is not particularly optimistic about the future. "Women have lost the habit of wearing hats, and they are a handicap for work and for our twentieth century's hurried lifestyle. Women of today are afraid of an accessory as obvious as a hat, and it would need a whole change in the way of thinking to reverse that trend." Meanwhile, Patrice Wolfer preserves and protects the heritage of Parisian millinery and watches over his stock of beautiful, exquisite things as though watching over a Sleeping Beauty, in the hope that people's love of exquisite millinery will, once again, awaken again one day and flourish as in decades gone by.

La Sainte Catherine

Millinery is full of quaint little customs, stories, and superstitions which have been passed down through generations from *premières mains* (experienced milliners) to young apprentices just starting to learn the art of hatmaking. A shared heritage of this kind contributes greatly to the bond in the close intimacy of small workrooms, or *ateliers*, as they are called in Paris.

One of the traditions is the celebration of Saint Catherine, the patron saint of milliners, whose feast day falls on November 27. The story of Saint Catherine has its origins in fourth-century Sinai, where Africa meets Asia. A beautiful and intelligent girl, Catherine studied philosophy, something

A tied scarf/turban design made from the new "wet look" fabric, a forerunner to the vast range of new synthetic fabrics

IS THIS JUST ANOTHER FAD?

The big beret.

12s 6d.

12 Quant colours.

Enquiries
for Quant berets
to
39 Fitzroy
Square,
London W1.

MARY QUANT

▌Youthful styles by Mary Quant accessorized by the casual look of a soft beret

1990–2000

1980–1990

1970–1980

1960–1970

1950–1960

1940–1950

1930–1940

1920–1930

1910–1920

1900–1910

Disillusion and Flower Power

THE SIXTIES YOUTH REBELLION WAS FOLLOWED BY A DECADE OF disillusion in the 1970s. Martin Luther King, Jr., had been assassinated in April 1968, and just two months later, Attorney General Robert Kennedy met the same fate as his brother, John. The Vietnam War, the longest and most unpopular conflict in American history, raged, causing ill feelings among friendly nations as well as seriously demoralizing US armed forces. Anti-war demonstrations all over the Western world brought the withdrawal of American troops in 1973 and the end of the war in 1975.

Across the Atlantic, Britain was rife with strikes, industrial unrest, power cuts, and high inflation. France was recovering after the May 1968 student uprising, which provoked a conservative backlash. The younger generation hit back with militant feminism, symbolized by burning bras, and by rejecting mainstream culture in favor of alternative hippie lifestyles.

Fashion is Dead—Long Live Style!

The Seventies fashion scene was a diverse mixture of styles. Ethnic influences created a colorful picture; gypsy skirts, mystic cotton robes, and thrift-shop clothes were all part of the anti-establishment protests. This "anti-fashion" expressed itself in the multicolored, many textured and layered look, accessorized with handcrafted decorations, ethnic jewelry, and symbols of peace. Underwear was unrestrictive and minimal, underlining the trend for natural living and the rural dream of communes, where young people grew vegetables, baked bread, and supported themselves with handicrafts, embroidery, and knitting. British designer Laura

Graham Smith

LONDON'S MASTER MILLINER

Charming, elegant, and authoritative, Graham Smith is London's undisputed master of millinery, a position he has held since the 1960s. He admits that understanding his clients, their social calendar, and the needs of different lifestyles and social occasions is the key to his enduring success and has taken years to perfect. He also graciously attributes his success to a number of mentors, who taught him so much when he was young.

Born in London, Graham Smith studied fashion design in the mid-1950s, then specialized in millinery at the Royal College of Art. Even before graduating, he was called to Paris to work for the design house Lanvin-Castillo, and spent the night of his 21st birthday making hats until two o'clock in the morning. This might have been an omen for his future life, as he admits to still working long hours and weekends when an important client or event requires his skills.

Returning to London, he associated himself with Michael of Carlos Place, a member of the Incorporated Society of London Fashion Designers, an organisation which promoted *haute couture* in London. Graham Smith became their resident hat designer for the next seven years. Setting up his own business in 1967, he was well qualified to design for clients in high society as well as actresses of stage and screen. Actress Elizabeth Taylor used to love coming to London, always staying at the Dorchester Hotel, and choosing from Graham's designs. He would send over a box of 10 hats, usually only getting one back, as she would often keep all the others. Showbusiness star Barbra Streisand was another devotee, once Graham Smith understood the particular style of turban she wanted.

It is not surprising to find out that Graham Smith's favorite *couturiers* are Balenciaga and Givenchy, something which is much reflected in his style. His model hats

▮ Smith's model hats are unmistakable in their elegant proportions, witty decoration, and quality of workmanship. These fine exotic straw brims with crowns overflowing with artificial flowers, are perfect examples of his work

are outstanding for their elegant, flattering shapes and proportions as well as for originality in design. Graham Smith's clients love the detailed craftsmanship as well as the personal touch of including one or two matching hatpins with each model hat, as it is lovingly packed with lots of tissue paper into a box. Graham is a perfectionist and checks every hat before it goes out, often spending time adjusting the trimmings of the Graham Smith II ready-to-wear range.

Graham Smith is also an expert in mass-market hats. He became in-house designer for Kangol in 1981 and was consultant design director until 1998. Since the end of his long association, which put Kangol very much on the map as hat designers for the young, Graham has been appointed millinery consultant for Bhs, a British chain store group.

His feelings about the future of millinery are that fashion is confused. "From having been orderly with twice-a-year collections that gave women directions in style, publicity has taken over fashion," he says. "Shows have become theatrical and are not what women want to wear. There is a much smaller market for millinery today, and yet women buy hats for the love of them. Hats are special occasion wear, they are for weddings, royal garden parties, and Ascot, because in the general scheme, dress has become so casual." There is certainly nothing casual about a hat by Graham Smith.

▌A fine transparent straw hat from the
Graham Smith British Home Stores
ready-to-wear collection

111

Far left: Cinnamon sued[e]
a saffron ziggurat prin[t]
jacket with collar, flaps, b[?]
binding a black and gold
suede. Scorpic's skirt fa[ll]
suede pleats, big and [?]
£92. Suede boots in that [?]
to order, The Chelsea C[obbler]
Sundance kid suede hat, [?]
tian Dior London. Silver[?]
buckled up in black che[?]
Ido Davidson, Thea Porte[?]
Honey pigskin dress, [?]
with black and milk cho[?]
Tight bodice, a deep yoke[?]
ing stitched pleats which [?]
from the waist. The fulle[?]
you've seen, knifed into [?]
of jersey and tweed check[?]
Both by Bill Gibb for Ba[?]
far left, at Loewe; Edna [?]
Harrogate; left, Harvey N[?]
31 Shop. Watch, Cartie[?]
son, Otto Lucas, printed [?]
carat. Suede fringe bag, [?]
Mann. Hair, Oliver at L[?]

*v*et ANCIENT AND MODERN,
FLAME AND BLACK,
WHAT MORE BEAUTIFUL

Flame velvet antique dress from
Afghanistan, *left:* beautifully aged
and richly sewn with loops and
twirls of golden braid. £40, at Oxus.
Black and orange Persian silk scarf
trailing from under the hat, 6 gns,
at Mr Fish. Purple suede boots on
purple snake feet, 32 gns, to order,
The Chelsea Cobbler. Liquid black
panne velvet knickerbockers, *right:*
slender ones with chiffon shirt, all
loose and gathered in, and soft with
velvet spots shimmering flame,
saffron, black. By Graham Price,
£14 10s, £46 7s. 6d, at Chic of
Hampstead. Chiffon and velvet
shawl afloat with roses, silver-
green and bronze, deep silk fringes,
£12 10s, The Purple Shop, Chelsea
Antique Market. Black tights, by
Wolford, 13s, Fenwick. Black silk
ghillies, by Dior, £20, at Charles
Jourdan. Feather cockade and
leather ribbons, by Pablo & Delia,
£16, Thea Porter. Black silk roses,
19s. 11d each, cherries, from range,
D.H. Evans. Hair, Oliver at Leonard.
Sizes and colours, see Stockists

The multicoloured, multilayered, flowing look of the 1970s, styled with hats for a special occasion. Photographs for *Vogue* 1970

Ashley started her business in this way, producing country-style smocks, romantic frilly blouses, and pretty home decorations.

Both men and women wore their hair long, curled or straight, but most important it had to look unkempt and wild. Blow-drying took over from tight perms and hours spent with curlers under hooded hair dryers. As for hats, structured, conventional styles were rejected, and droopy cloches and pull-on berets became popular with the younger generation. London's teen shops were selling simple, unblocked hoods in felt or straw, trimmed with *macramé* braids, leather bands, and buckles, or just one romantic flower for decoration. The older generation and the increasing number of working women did not join in the "flower power" look; they wanted more conventional classics. This style was provided by Bill Blass, Ralph Lauren, and Calvin Klein in the United States, Jean Muir in Britain, and Yves Saint Laurent in France. Paris *haute couture* suffered during the hippie years. Only Yves Saint Laurent had the foresight to combine *couture* with ready-to-wear. His successful *Rive Gauche* line identified his designs with the ideas of young students on the Left Bank of the River Seine.

New influences came from Japan, with Issey Miyake and French-trained Kenzo.

Italian designers put Milan on the fashion map. Designer Vivienne Westwood in London was the great news on the *avant-garde* horizon, creating ageless, classless, anarchic clothes, which revolutionized established fashion concepts in the future.

Floppy Hats and the Layered Look

Millinery, like *couture*, had a difficult time, but a few designers held their own in London and in Paris, by adapting the concept of uncluttered, clean designs. It was not easy for

A young woman at Ascot wearing her elaborate scarecrow-style Seventies straw hat with frayed brim

1990-2000

1980-1990

1970-1980

1960-1970

1950-1960

1940-1950

1930-1940

1920-1930

1910-1920

1900-1910

Jean-Charles Brosseau

MODERN HATS WITH A WHIFF OF NOSTALGIA

Casual soft hats were very much in demand during the 1970s and Jean-Charles Brosseau turned the drafting of flat patterns for floppy brims and berets into an art form. Like Graham Smith in London, he had a solid *couture* apprenticeship with Jacques Fath and had started his career very young. He recognized the change in the mood of society in the 1960s and 1970s and saw the future of hats as a practical, flattering accessory, which should be sporty and easy to wear.

Brosseau's elegant hat shop opened in 1970, on a corner of Place des Victoires, Paris. He also designed hats for Kenzo, a near neighbor, and widened his range to include fashion accessories, like gloves, umbrellas, and handbags, adding to the success of the business. In 1977, he felt that there was only one thing missing from the Brosseau range, a perfume, which he believed was an indispensable accessory for men or women.

Brosseau tells the story of his perfume *Ombre Rose* in his gentle, self-deprecating style, suggesting that its success may have been accidental. The creation of a unisex scent called *Bross-Eau* had served as Brosseau's apprenticeship in the art of perfume making. For years, he had dreamed of finding a perfect perfume for women of any age, at any time of day, and for any occasion. In his mind were childhood memories of the Anjou region of France, when aunts sitting on lush, silky sofas would take him on their knees. He never forgot that feeling of comfort and well-being combined with that wonderful smell of face powder mingled with scent.

By sheer accident, he found it again. It was a moment of instant recognition, like having found a long-lost love. *Ombre Rose* (Shadow of Roses)—a mixture of rosewood, honey, lily of the valley, roses, and sandalwood—was born. The perfect container—an old bottle from the 1920s, with a charming stylized flower design —was found in a glass factory in Normandy. There were no name or initials, the shape and design of the bottle was to be Brosseau's signature.

Being known to the American stores for his hats helped Brosseau with connections to the world of perfume distribution. Success came swiftly; Bergdorf Goodman in New York sold 2,300 bottles in 14 days! *Ombre Rose* was followed by *Ombre Bleu* and *Ombre d'Or*. A childhood memory had been transformed into a commercial reality.

▌*top* Clean cut elegance was Brosseau's hallmark and won him acclaim in America

▌*above* His beret made from easycare fabrics could be rolled up and carried like an umbrella without losing its chic and elegance

▌*above* Jean-Charles Brosseau the Parisian milliner with a vision for the future, designed uncluttered hats for the modern Seventies woman. Pictured here is his sun-ray pleat fine straw with a swept-up brim, inspired by Japanese *origami* designs

▌*left* Brosseau's version of a sleek straw trilby trimmed with seashells which could be worn with the new casual fashion for flared slacks for women

by his patient wife, is trying to find the right cap. He tries one on, feels it, clutches it, molds it to his head, and compares it to another. It seems as if that he is choosing a best friend. The assistant is helpful and reassuring, quietly explaining the detailed nuances of tweed caps, seeming more like a butler in a stately home than a sales assistant. The rush and hustle of the world outside just would not be appropriate at James Lock.

Lock & Co. dates back to 1676, when George James Lock was granted the lease of the premises in St James's Street. Continuing with his grandson James Lock I and consequent generations of James Locks, the present chairman is N. C. Lock McDonald, a descendent of this family of hatters.

The reputation of the company was built on traditional hard hats for gentlemen and it was Mr Lock who had asked Mr Bowler to design the most famous of all hats, the black bowler or coke, as Mr Lock used to call it, after the client who commissioned it rather than the maker. The older top hats, which are referred to as black silk plushes, are the most precious stock and are kept in a backroom of the shop. No new ones are now produced, but Lock's offers a renovating service for family heirlooms.

hats to blend in with the ever changing mini, midi, and maxi skirt lengths. With designers like Graham Smith, Frederick Fox, Simone Mirman, Reed Crawford, Dolores, and Mitzi Lorenz, London held its own.

The millinery factories in Luton, an historic hatmaking town 30 miles north of London, contributed to the boom in inexpensive hats by producing a variety of ready-to-wear ranges. Bermona Hats, Marida, and Kangol established quality mass production of hats and exported their styles all over Europe and America. Traditional millinery might have been in decline, but hats were still in business.

Three Centuries of Tradition

Most men stopped wearing hats during the 1960s and have remained hatless since, something much regretted by many women who find men with hats simply irresistible. According to the originator of psychoanalysis, Sigmund Freud, hats are an extension of masculinity. Fashion analyst and historian, James Laver, expands on this theory, comparing the height of a man's hat to his standing in society. If he is to be believed, men's status has altered

significantly since top hats were popular.

The staff of James Lock & Co., right in the heart of London's gentleman's club land would not agree and feel that men's hats are very much alive and well. The establishment of Lock's, Gentlemen's Hatters, has been in the same premises for over 300 years and has served the world with toppers, bowlers, panamas, and shooting caps, not forgetting the **smoking hat**, a velvet cap with a silk tassel, for an evening by the fireside.

The quaint shop in St James's Street conveys an atmosphere of great comfort and charm. Customers are greeted with courteous warmth and discreet politeness. It feels as much like a place to take afternoon tea in as one for buying a hat. The shop oozes tradition, with rows of white, shiny hatboxes containing shiny, silk plush hats or bowlers proudly display the name Lock & Co. in elegant black lettering. Colonial safari helmets stand around the fireplace and tweed caps of every size and variety are stacked in pigeon-hole shelves. Grouse caps are bought for hunting, walking, and fishing, but some people prefer the Minsmere cap, which is named after a wildlife area of Suffolk, a county in eastern England.

The shop is humming and pleasantly busy. A man, accompanied

1990–2000

1980–1990

1970–1980

1960–1970

1950–1960

1940–1950

1930–1940

1920–1930

1910–1920

1900–1910

LOCK & Cº.
HATTERS.
S.James's Street.
LONDON.
FOUNDED 1676

above and opposite A selection of the current range in men's hats by Lock & Co. Apart from the traditional silk toppers and stiff felt bowlers, Lock & Co. offers a variety of tweed hats, check deerstalkers with visors and ear flaps, fine straw panamas, hard safari hats, and soft velvet smoking caps with silk tassels

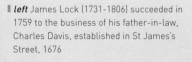

Sizing a man's hat is taken very seriously at Lock & Co. as the fitting makes all the difference between a hat looking dashing or ridiculous. The contraption which helps to achieve a perfect fit is called a *conformateur* and was invented by a Frenchman in the mid-nineteenth century. This ingenious invention of movable wooden pegs can map the exact contour of the skull, which is transferred to a piece of card, then named, dated, and stored. If a hat needs to be fitted for a customer, the card is located, and the shape is transferred to the block. The block is then inserted into the fitting of a hat, which

has been heated so that it sets to the individual head shape as it cools down. Lock's have thousands of cards, recording the shapes and headsizes of past and present customers. The drawers are like secret files and contain the confidential head details of many famous clients, like Charlie Chaplin, General de Gaulle, Frank Sinatra, Sir Alec Guinness, and Paul McCartney. Even the measurements of Lord Lucan, an English aristocrat who disappeared mysteriously some years ago after allegedly killing his children's nanny, are carefully filed away. A clever scientist may one day make a study of the skull shapes on the cards, and who

knows what the analysis might reveal?

Lock & Co. is like a secret island, untouched by the pressures of modern life. There are no cash tills, credit card machines, price tags, or piped music. Janet Taylor, who deals with public relations, admits to one or two computers upstairs in the accounts department looking quite alien and out of place. Orders are handwritten in a huge ledger, which looks something like a family Bible. Each finished volume is alphabetically numbered. This is part of the ethos of Lock & Co. Hatters, with traditions of the past that will stay well into the future.

Frederick Fox

DIVINE BRETONS FROM A ROYAL MILLINER

Freddie Fox, as his friends call him, has been an established name on the British millinery scene since 1964, when he opened his first salon in London's Brook Street. More than 30 years later, elegant and charming with silver-gray hair, sparkling blue eyes, and a lot of common sense, he is still very much in charge at his London's Bond Street salon.

The list of Fox clients over the years is an illustrious one, including actress Shirley MacLaine, and society ladies Ira von Fürstenberg, the Duchess of York, and the Duchess of Kent. Some would come to order as many as a dozen hats for a season. Margaret, Duchess of Argyle, who was one of the "professional beauties" of the 1930s and a loyal customer for 35 years, simply could not live without Mr Fox's divine bretons. He remembers having made over 100 different versions of the style which became very much his speciality.

Frederick Fox's bretons with upturned brims in all their variations were very flattering and combined femininity, an uncluttered line, and timeless elegance. Hillary Clinton recognized this when she chose a blue velour hat by Frederick Fox for the day when her husband was inaugurated as President of the United States in January 1993.

The flair for making women look beautiful dates back to Freddie's childhood in the outback of southern New South Wales, Australia, where he grew up with four older sisters. He loved drawing and looking at the Australian *Women's Weekly* magazine and amused himself by changing around

❙ *above left* A chinchilla fur beret, the most precious fur used for millinery during the 1960s

❙ *above right* Exotic straw cloche trimmed with an array of flowers and romantic white veiling

trimmings on his mother's hats when he was only 12 years old. This talent was very much appreciated by his sisters and their friends and led to the making of whole hats as soon as rationing was finished after World War II and it was possible to get fabrics and materials again. At 17, Freddie Fox left home for Sydney to learn millinery formally at J.L. Normoyle, a large hat company and factory, where he stayed for nine years.

Leaving Australia in 1958, Freddie went to Paris, then on to London, where Otto Lucas, who always had an eye for talented newcomers, offered him a job. This did not last very long and Frederick Fox remembers Otto Lucas as a difficult boss. Three years at Mitzi Lorenz followed, and having learned the finer points of millinery, he joined Madame Langée in Brook Street, taking over her salon a few years later. A meeting with Hardy Amies, the Queen's designer, led to Frederick Fox becoming the youngest milliner to make hats for the British Queen. He was also the longest lasting, in a series of hat designers who have served Her Majesty over the years.

With such an illustrious career behind him, Frederick Fox is optimistic about the future of hats, but not very hopeful for expensive and exclusive design. "Jeans and baseball caps will evolve from the comfort of wearing a uniform-orientated kit," he says in a tone of pragmatic resignation. "Hats will be one way of putting an individual signature on dress." When asked about his wider thoughts about millinery, he muses: "Millinery can be an art form if one is rich, it's a craft if one wants to eat." Frederick Fox has achieved both.

▌*left* A deep turban draped in angora jersey

▌*above* Frederick Fox is renowned for his flair and his traditional craftsmanship. Over 30 years of experience in the business has made him a master of millinery, admired by his faithful clientele as well as by young students from fashion colleges, who often join his staff on work experience. Pictured here is one of his sophisticated "Garbo" cloches trimmed with waxed cotton camelias

The Panama

SHADY ELEGANCE

A real Montecristi panama is the finest straw hat in the world and the most expensive one. Costing several hundred dollars, it can only be obtained at a few distinguished hatters, such as J.J. Hat Center in New York, Lock & Co. or Herbert Johnson in London, and at Gelot in Paris. This exclusive and costly headgear is produced by some of the very poorest people in the world who handweave the hats in villages on the plains of Ecuador. Time seems to stand still in this remote part of Latin America, where pride and poverty have always been intertwined.

Today there remain few weavers with the skills of making a Montecristi *superfino*, the finest of all the ivory-colored panama hats. This connoisseur's hat is recognized by the superb subtleness, elasticity, and density of the weave. An experienced weaver could take four to six months to make one hat and will be paid about one-tenth of the retail price of the hat.

Weavers work the *toquilla* straw fibers with their skillful fingers at dawn and again at dusk, as the heat of the day would make the straw too brittle. A few miles away from their bamboo houses built on stilts are the lush *toquilla* plantations where the raw material for making panama hats is grown. The fan-shaped tops of the plants are harvested according to the phases of the moon, which are said to affect the pliability of the straw. The three-foot-long shoots are split with knives into fine strips, which are then boiled in earthenware pots and wind dried for two days. Traditionally, the long straw fringes are smoked with sulfur to enhance the delicate ivory color. This basic procedure has not changed for centuries.

The weaving starts from the "flower" at the top of the hat and takes shape row after row into the form of a hood. The artisan's great skill, passed on from generation to generation, is to weave using three fingers of each hand, separating the strands with long, pointed fingernails. The art of weaving hats may have originated among the Native American people who showed their woven headgear to the Spanish conquerors over 400 years ago. The straw hats were called *jipijapas* which was changed to *toquillas*, after *toques*, the name for the hats the Spanish invaders wore. Montecristi is the name of the place where the finest panama hats are made.

The hats were named panamas after the shipping port, where merchants sold hats to the arriving gold prospectors and shipped thousands of hats to the United States and Europe. In the eighteenth century, Panama was an important trading center for South America. Ships laden with gold, sugar, coffee, and cacao sailed from the port of Guayaquil, a major port in Ecuador, to Panama, and the first *toquilla* hats might well have traveled to the Old World in sea-captains' baggage.

Both Ecuador and Panama benefited from the trade in hats. The old weaver's saying "gone to Panama" refers to the dead, who, like the hats for Panama, never come

▌Members of a local family handweave panama straw hats in front of their house in Cuenca, Ecuador

back again. By the middle of the nineteenth century, 500,000 hats were exported every year from Ecuador. The start of construction on the Panama Canal in 1900 prompted a new wave of publicity. American president Theodore Roosevelt wore a Montecristi when he inspected the construction project in 1906, and made the Panama canal and the hat front-page news.

King Edward VII of Britain, who was known for his interest in fashion, had a Montecristi made at Robert Gelot in Paris and a *fino-fino* panama was shown at the World Fair in 1900. The great advantage was that it could be folded in half, rolled up and stored in a small wooden box, not much larger than a pencil case. With a flip of the hand the hat sprang back into shape again, and even today, it has an enduring attraction for many people. Traveling to different cities in Europe and beyond was a new form of entertainment for higher social classes in the first decade of the twentieth century. The panama was an ideal travel companion and looked equally at ease in London, Berlin, Monte Carlo, or Cairo.

To the chagrin of the very rich the original panama was copied, allowing dandies of all social classes to buy inexpensive versions from Cuenca, another city in Ecuador, as well as Borsalino hats from Italy. True lovers of Panamas never let themselves be lured into such disloyalty. A genuine Montecristi *fino-fino* is a refined touch for a gentleman wearing a light-colored linen suit, brogues, and smoking a fine cigar.

In the first half of the century, Cuba was renowned for elegant men with great zest for life and was the best market for Panama hats. This irresistible masculine elegance was imitated by a number of Hollywood's male glamor actors in the 1940s. Orson Welles, Humphrey Bogart, Gary Cooper, and Charlton Heston conveyed this elegant yet strongly masculine look. The 1971 film *Death in Venice*, directed by Italian film director Luchino Visconti, gave the hat a sad and nostalgic image. British actor Dirk Bogarde portrayed an aging Von Aschenbach desperately trying to regain his lost youth.

The hatless postwar period and competition from straw hat manufacturers in Italy, the Far East, and China was bad news for the hat weavers of Ecuador. American President John F. Kennedy represented bareheaded liberalism to the world, but Soviet Union's Secretary-General Nikita Khrushchev loved panamas. He showed his more liberal, anti-Stalin opinions by wearing his Montecristi whenever the sun was shining. Despite this vote for the panama hat from the Soviet head of state, the decline of the Panama industry further accelerated when Ecuador broke off diplomatic relations with the United States during the Cuban missile crisis in 1962. This resulted in a 75 percent reduction in the panama trade, from which it never recovered. Skilled straw weavers had to find different ways of earning their living, and the younger generation saw no future in learning the ancient skills of their grandfathers.

Despite this, the "prince of hats" seems to hold the secret of eternal youth. The many pairs of hands needed to make one hat, and the stroking of each strand of *toquilla* straw before it is densely woven gives a Montecristi hat a lifespan easily as long as a precious Persian carpet. A panama hat also improves with the years, even if the patina of age renders the straw more honey-colored and less bright than in the spring of its youth.

top The panama is a hat for light-hearted gentlemen. Its honey-colored flexible straw protects against the sun on elegant summer occasions

above A true panama hat can be folded and rolled to fit in a small tube box

Conspicuous Consumption

THE 1980s WAS A PERIOD OF RELATIVE PEACE AND STABILITY IN THE Western world, where solid conservatism was the rule. In America, Ronald Reagan reestablished American confidence after the Watergate years. Across the Atlantic, Mrs Thatcher, the "Iron Lady," restored order to the British economy. Communism crumbled in the Soviet bloc. On November 10, 1989, the Berlin Wall came down, an event which finally relegated World War II and its aftermath to history and opened up the opportunity for a larger European Union.

From Punk to Power Dressing

Fashion offered a wide range of expression to men and women, ranging from anarchic punk to sleek power dressing. Designers in New York, Paris, London, and Milan created many different styles, lines, and movements, and fresh, talented influences from Japan, like Yohji Yamamoto and Rei Kawakubo for Comme des Garçons, contributed *avant-garde* ideas and futuristic thinking.

Hemlines rose again, starting with rah-rah skirts over woolen tights, flat-heeled boots, and legwarmers in the early 1980s to become straight and aggressively short miniskirts in the middle years of the decade. The fitness craze had started; sports clothes introduced a casual style in dressing, with easywear jogging suits, sweatshirts, leggings, and trainers.

New York, Paris, and Milan offered high-class chic with sharp day-time tailoring for the career woman. Dark-colored, masculine-style suits with large shoulder pads were women's passports into the men's world. The trend was known as power dressing.

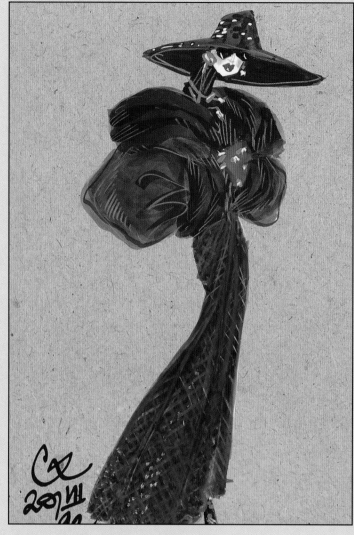

Glamorous hats and clothing by Christian Lacroix, the master of ornate, opulent chic. His flamboyant costume jewelry and vibrant colors inspired the return of *couture* fashion design in the extravagant Eighties

Glamorous femininity was relegated to the evening, with puffball gowns, gilt and silver decorations, and fantastic jewelry, reaching sumptuous proportions with Christian Lacroix's debut label on the fashion scene. This "big bucks" look, as the *International Herald Tribune* called it, coincided incidentally, and perhaps ironically, with the stockmarket crash of 1987.

Living in a Material World

Soap operas were taking over the glamor role that Hollywood had filled in the 1940s and 1950s. The dress influences of TV programs like *Dallas* and *Dynasty* were clearly seen and actresses like Joan Collins as Alexis and Linda Gray as Sue Ellen portrayed images of powerful women who became role models for many on both sides of the Atlantic. They were dressed by clever *couturiers* like Yves Saint Laurent in Paris and Calvin Klein in New York, who seized the opportunity and created the required style of luxurious minimalism.

Madonna, the inventor of the "material girl" image, became the idol of the very young as well as the yuppies' dream woman. Regularly breaking social taboos, many of Madonna's radically sexy and outrageous outfits were created by French designer Jean-Paul Gaultier and they delighted the world's media as well as her publicity machine. London's fashion message of the era was new romanticism, referred to as "young, anarchic chic" by British *Vogue*. Vivienne Westwood, a British designer of unlimited imagination and wit, presented witches' clothes with graffiti in 1983, fluorescent bodysuits in 1984, and a collection of "mini-crinnies" (mini crinolines) in 1985, as a caricature of the 1980s mood of conspicuous consumption.

Stephen Jones, the New Romantic milliner, created hats for his friend and client Boy George, whose style of dress was a visual expression of his philosophy of wanting to create an ideal "culture club" world. The other promising name in millinery was a young graduate from the London College of Fashion, Kirsten Woodward, who made surreal armchair hats and went on to become

Princess Diana

HATS FIT FOR A PRINCESS

Millinery did not regain the status it had enjoyed during the first half of the century, but the more sophisticated look of the Eighties offered a great opportunity for hats. The required female image of this decade was not girlish anymore, it was mature, womanly, with clothes and hats to be taken seriously.

In the summer of 1981, Lady Diana Spencer became both the Princess of Wales and the fashion icon of the decade. Everyone wanted to see her and photographs of her graced glossy magazines around the world. On her busy schedule of official functions and overseas tours, the world's press and the public could not wait to see which outfit she would unveil next. She loved hats and looked wonderful in many different styles expressing different occasions, moods, and stages in her life. As a very young "shy Di," little riding hats were perfect. Upswept brims and bretons framed her radiant face when she became a mother a few years later. She looked sleek and chic when she wore stylish, wide-brimmed matador-style hats, and she hid her face under large-brimmed cloches, on the sadder occasions of her life. For London's milliners she was truly heaven sent; nobody could have wished for a more elegant, sophisticated, and glamorous ambassadress for the hat industry.

John Boyd was Diana's first milliner, having served her mother for many years. He created the early styles of small hats and the little tricorn riding hat in apricot straw, trimmed with ostrich plumes, which she wore with her going-away outfit after her wedding. Graham Smith was another favorite. He remembers the charming white cotton sailor hat that Diana wore visiting a Royal Navy ship on an official visit to Italy. She also called on Frederick Fox, and discovered hats by Marina Killery, a newcomer to millinery in the early 1990s.

❙ Diana, Princess of Wales and ambassador for hats, on a royal visit to Germany dressed in navy blue and white with a matching hat by Philip Somerville

Philip Somerville

CHARM BY APPOINTMENT

Though born in England, Philip Somerville has childhood roots in New Zealand. From there he moved to Australia, where he became a stage actor, later establishing his career in millinery in London in the Sixties and Seventies. His elegant, uncomplicated, and stylish hats are appreciated by a wide clientele of society ladies as well as by women who just enjoy dropping into his shop. Philip Somerville, tall, silver-haired, and handsome, looks after them with quiet charm and warmth. His clients know they can trust his eye for style.

Life in London started in 1961, when he arrived on leave of absence from his job as a hat designer in Auckland. He had only planned to stay for six months, but he started to work for Otto Lucas and has been in England ever since.

Otto Lucas, working out of London's New Bond Street, was a great influence and the association was beneficial for both of them. "Somerville," as Mr Lucas used to call him, became the company's front man. Otto Lucas was not always good at handling customers, and Philip Somerville, with his relaxed sense of style and elegance, was able to charm even the most demanding buyers. As a result sales figures doubled at the New Bond Street shop in just a few seasons.

▌A red felt breton trimmed with the tweed fabric from Her Majesty's suit and edged with gold braid

A business of his own came in 1972, after Otto Lucas's death. Moving around the corner from Bond Street to smaller premises, Philip took some of the Otto Lucas workforce with him and retained Miss Jolly, Mr Lucas's former business manager. All of the first collection, a mixture of the Otto Lucas "classic look" and his own ideas, was bought up by Harrods, the famous London department store. Saks, Lord and Taylor, and Bergdorf Goodman department stores of New York followed as important clients. With a thriving wholesale business, Philip Somerville expanded, gradually taking over a whole building. In 1986, an elegant salon and retail shop opened on the first floor, frequented by an illustrious clientele from film, stage, society, and the aristocracy.

Recognizable by their simplicity, elegance, and style, Somerville hats were brought to the attention of the Princess of Wales, who saw one on a TV news report. She asked her hairdresser to find out about the hat stylist and to pave the way for her first visit. She loved coming to the shop, which also amused her son, Prince William. Accompanying her there once he gave a little note saying: "Thank you for making Mummy such beautiful hats."

The royal visits to the hat salon became known and attracted an ever intrusive crowd of photographers. The whole world wanted to see the Princess, and she accompanied Prince Charles on many foreign tours during the 1980s, needing hats to go with different outfits. Making hats for Diana was a joy and privilege for Philip Somerville; her warmth, generosity, and informality was often touching. The Christmas cards and small, thoughtful gifts that she sent are things that he treasures.

Philip Somerville was awarded the Royal Warrant in 1994, which hangs in a place of honor in his shop. He is proud of this achievement and likes to share it with his loyal team whom he likes to call "the children." He has been making hats for Queen Elizabeth for several years; not always an easy task because not only must they look right and please Her Majesty, they must also placate the media, who complain if a hat overshadows the monarch's face.

Philip Somerville is always honored when he is called to Buckingham Palace, but he enjoys the personal contact with all his clients. Whether it is the extravagant and perfectionist Joan Collins, New Zealand opera star Kiri Te Kanawa, Susan Sangster, wife of racehorse millionaire Robert Sangster, or the stars of the latest James Bond film, they come to his salon to find just the right hat.

▮ Philip Somerville, milliner to Queen Elizabeth II, photographed in his studio surrounded by the tools of his trade and designing a new model hat for Her Majesty, pictured opposite in the finished article

1990–2000

1980–1990

1970–1980

1960–1970

1950–1960

1940–1950

1930–1940

1920–1930

1910–1920

1900–1910

designer Karl Lagerfeld's favorite milliner. Young British designers were at the forefront of new ideas and rising star, John Galliano, who had recently graduated from London's St Martin's College of Art with a degree show entitled *Les Incroyables* (The Unbelievables), drew the attention of the international fashion press to London.

Gentlemen Hatters

The Worshipful Company of Feltmakers of London is an ancient and traditional livery company, dating back to 1501, when it embraced hatters, furriers, and haberdashers in one guild. Guilds were medieval associations of craftsmen and merchants, whose aim was to protect their professions, to nurture young apprentices and to look after those who could no longer work.

The quest for a separate guild of hatters dates back to the reign of Queen Elizabeth I, when 7,000 hatters working in the City of London petitioned the queen to grant them independence from their fellow guild members, the haberdashers, whom they accused of dishonest dealings, by selling inferior raw materials for making hats. It took another hundred years before the first Master of the Wardens of "The Art or Mystery of Feltmakers of London" took up his post and wore, for the first time, the elaborate black tricorn felt hat, trimmed with white feathers, as a symbol of his office.

The function of the guild today is to preserve a link with the past, provide sponsorship for young designers, and support old and poor hatters with an income from the benevolent fund. The annual hat design competition is a highlight in the curriculum of many fashion design colleges in Britain. The winner of the first prize not only enjoys a financial award but is invited to the Feltmakers' annual dinner, a traditional and sumptuous evening at the Mansion House, the official residence of the Lord Mayor of London.

Every year in November, when the City of London welcomes its new Lord Mayor, he is ceremoniously presented with a hat by the Feltmakers. After his year in office, he has to return the famous red cloak, but keeps his

❚ *Decus et Tutamen*, the Latin for "Cover and Protection," is the inscription on the crest of the Worshipful Company of Feltmakers of London

hat as a gift from the Worshipful Feltmakers.

Bill Horsman, Third Warden of this ancient guild, has also been Chairman of the British Hat Guild, a newer trade association, since 1978. Besides these honorary positions, he runs a successful wholesale hat company in Luton, England, producing 200,000 hats a year, including exports to the United States, Europe, and Australia.

A philanthropist, Bill Horsman likes to support the development of millinery and has not forgotten the financial difficulties facing young, talented designers. Financial sponsorship to the Royal College of Art in London, from where he graduated, enabled a

millinery course to be set up in 1988. Philip Treacy, the brightest new talent in London, benefited from Horsman's support when he set up his own business in 1991. This generous gesture enabled Treacy to climb the ladder of fashion fame, and did a great service to the millinery industry as a whole.

The latest Bill Horseman venture is designing and manufacturing hats in the Far East, and he regularly travels to China to teach and supervise hat production. With his eye on the future and his love of the past, Bill Horsman is guided by the same vision as his predecessors of the Worshipful Company of Feltmakers, 400 years ago.

Stephen Jones

ROMANTICALLY MAD ABOUT HATS

Hat designers have always been rather unusual and interesting characters, but Stephen Jones, 1980s *enfant terrible*, tops them all. Meeting him in his light, airy shop in London's Covent Garden leaves an impression of a highly articulate, courteous, and soft-spoken counselor, rather than a hat designer. A good listener, interested in other people, Stephen talks about fashion in a clear, analytical way. His twinkling brown eyes reveal humanity, wit, and a sense of humor which may seem surprising in an *avant-garde* rebel, but then, Stephen Jones was a rebel of the 1980s New Romantic era.

Stephen Jones did not consider millinery until he met Shirley Hex. She worked at Lachasse, the fashion house where Stephen did work experience during his college years. It was more Shirley's enthusiasm than millinery that ignited his passion for "solid constructed objects," as he refers to hats. As St Martin's College of Fashion did not have a millinery tutor, Stephen went to see Shirley in the morning before college and at lunchtimes and she helped him with his final collection as well as with a hat for his mother. When he turned up with 300 labels in a plastic bag, she told him he'd better start up his own business. Stephen remembers his mentor in those early days before his first shop in Endell Street, Covent Garden, a former vegetable market, transformed into a cluster of trendy London shops: "Shirley is like Buddha, when she says 'Do,' you do without question." Vivienne Westwood's "Mud Hat" was another great influence and so was her Punk Boutique called SEX on London's King's Road in the early 1980s.

Stephen's student years in London went way beyond college and fashion. London was full of colorful, interesting people who generated ideas and new lifestyles. New Romantics, as the press named the new dress-conscious posers, were defined as "punks with an addiction to the glamorous," by fashion analyst Ted Polhemus in his book *Street Styles*.

Stephen's first clients were all friends, wild and wacky young men like Boy George, Steve Strange, and Spandau Ballet, who dared to wear "visible accessories" for dressing up. Designing hats for his friends was good training as well as bringing much-needed publicity, because the fashion media did not accept Stephen Jones hats as a viable fashion trend. "*Vogue* wanted 'Prairie fashion' from Ralph Lauren and were not interested in wild young things. They wanted designs for Mrs Average, not Boy George."

When he opened his first salon in the trendy PX store at Covent Garden, London's *avant-garde* talked about it for weeks. Stephen Jones appeared in, and made the hats for Boy George's video, *Do you really want to hurt me?* and Jasper Conran, another friend, asked him to design hats for his catwalk show, which led to further contacts with the fashion world. Stephen Jones has developed a specialty of working with designers for catwalk shows, and collaborating with John Galliano, Claude Montana, Jean-Paul Gaultier, and Comme des Garçons, among others. As to how he copes with designers' reactions if his hats steal the limelight, Stephen Jones replies with a mellow smile of wisdom: "Blending in, yet standing out is the battle, it's hard work, but it's a friendly battle."

Stephen Jones' professional activities are directed from his latest hat salon in Great Queen Street, a few hundred yards from London's Royal Opera House. With its bright red runner carpet flanked by hats casually displayed on long perspex poles and tunes like *Mad about the Boy* by Dinah Washington, it is almost like walking the catwalk, with hats as spectators.

Jones' designs are an eclectic mix of discreet and wearable felts, fluffy marabou cloches in soft colors, and easy-to-wear tailored fabric caps. Sitting alone on one of the quaint little rococo tables is a *chapeau chasseur* in hard mirrored plastic, trimmed with a stark white ribbon. A black velvet mask hat with long bunny ears lined in pink satin peeps out from behind a tiny top hat with a face veil, one of Stephen Jones' unmistakable miniature frivolities. A charming modern-day chandelier with glass beads and miniature naked ladies in hats, acrobatically draping themselves around the halogen lights, hangs from the ceiling and illuminates the scene. With the morning sun pouring through the front door, the salon could almost be a stage set for Shakespeare's *The Tempest* with Ariel floating in at any moment.

The wild days of driving trucks by day and clubbing every night are now behind Stephen Jones. The growing awareness of Aids in the early Eighties changed his perspective on life and made him realize that career, success, and feeding his ego were not everything. However, he is driven on by his work, success, and his passion for hats. Apart from designer shows in Paris and model hats for private clients in London, he runs several diffusion ranges. "Miss Jones" and "Jonesboy" hats are made by his staff in London and "Jonesgirl" is produced under license in Japan with accessory ranges of scarves, kimonos, gloves, and sunglasses.

A down-to-earth New Romantic and a true Gemini, Stephen Jones is always interested in the new; fascinated by different cultures and happy working in a team. As to thoughts about the future, he is optimistic. "Heads will always be decorated, they always have been. Hats ultimately change the silhouette of the head, they express status and sexuality, and they are a tonic."

▮ Sculpted hat in purple silk and velvet by the master of new romantic millinery of the Eighties

The Stetson

WILD WEST STYLE FROM THE EAST COAST

Practical, protective, and synonymous with the West, the stetson is a truly American hat, combining function and style with a dashing air. A stetson is made for the outdoor life and needs the prairie winds to give it patina and a "battered" look. Not only does it protect a cowboy from the sun and the rain and keeps his hair free from dust, but a stetson can also be used to fan a fire, whip a horse, wave to a distant rider, and even become a makeshift bucket. For any cowboy, the stetson is an essential companion and best friend.

A genuine stetson is an object of quality and used to cost up to a month's wages. Even today a hat can cost as much as all the rest of the clothes in a Western outfit, and buying one is a serious investment. John Batterson Stetson's first prototype in 1865 sold for $5, but prices can reach $1,000 or more for a 10X beaver felt "Boss of the Plain." The "X" stands for the density of the fiber in the felt, which equals quality and durability.

His father, who was a hatter and had a business called No Name Hat Company in East Orange, Pennsylvania, taught all his 13 children the elementary principles of hatmaking. Suffering from tuberculosis and unfit for the Union Army, his son John went on a 750-mile trek on foot in search of fortune in the West. On the journey, he recovered his health and amused himself and his travel companions by felting fur from animal skins in front of the campfire. After soaking the animal hair shorn from the pelts, he kneaded the fibers and matted them again in a pot of hot water, creating a felt blanket, which he cut into a crude waterproof hat.

A passing cowboy liked it so much he gave Stetson a 5-dollar gold coin and rode off with the hat on his head. Stetson returned home to Philadelphia, without finding gold dust, but he struck true gold, making his fame and fortune with a hat company.

Hat production started in a rented room with two workers, and grew into a thriving business on the outskirts of Philadelphia, later to became the world's largest hat factory with 25 buildings spread over nine acres of ground. John B. Stetson was not only an ingenious entrepreneur, but also a caring, paternalistic employer with the interests of his workers at heart. His belief and motivation were rooted deeply in the Baptist religion and he provided housing, health care, and banking facilities for all his workers. Stetson was also a philanthropist, involving himself with the construction of a hospital, a fire station, and several Baptist chapels. His employees were offered 40 percent off the price of all merchandise and enjoyed extravagant Christmas parties.

Naturally they're STETSON HATS

❚ The stetson was conceived and created for the outdoor life of the prairies to protect its wearer from the extremes of weather

Modern production of stetsons is still based on the ancient principles of felting and hatmaking. Each hat goes through 13 stages, starting with the felting of the hoods, followed by the shaping and blocking of the hat, the finishing of the edges, the trimming of the outer headband, and the fitting of stampede strings, which will keep the hat on during the wildest rides and gustiest winds. Traditionally, the raw material for the felt was beaver or **nutria** fur, but rabbit hair and sheep's wool have become less expensive substitutes. A variety of textures are available: furry beaver, antelope, or pebble finishes. The popular colors, apart from black, are "silver belly" and "natural beaver."

The fitting is most important, for a hat which must look serious and trustworthy, be comfortable to wear, and stay firmly on the wearer's head. A perfect fit is achieved with the help of a *conformateur*, a French invention which records all the irregularities of the skull. The final stage is placing a fine leather sweatband around the inside of the crown to provide extra grip and increased comfort.

The body size of the wearer also has to be in harmony with the proportions of the hat. The height, the curl of the brim, as well as the creases and dents in the crown are all of paramount importance. Stetsons play a part in reinforcing the image of trustworthy hero, as well as reflecting masculinity and power.

Over the decades the image of the battered cowboy hat has mellowed and stylish stetsons have become fashion items and objects of fantasy. Any dedicated Western movie fan will remember Jack Mahoney, Glenn Ford, and especially Tim McCoy wearing a Monster Peak stetson. Gary Cooper, who liked to play morally upright men engaged in lone fights for justice, added strength to his cause with his hats. Steve McQueen was convincing wearing a stetson in 1960s TV show *Wanted Dead or Alive*, and in 1985, Clint Eastwood wore a flat-crowned cowboy hat in *Pale Rider* seeking just revenge for the rape of his wife.

The fashion in cowboy hats prompted diversification of the classic stetson. New companies like Bailey Hats, Rand's, and the Az-Tex Hat Company joined this lucrative market. The latest addition in 1980 was Charlie 1 Horse, which provides novelty with custom-designed cowboy hats, delivered in a wooden coffin-shaped, satin-lined box. A Charlie 1 Horse hat is instantly recognizable by its dominant front decorations of rattlesnake skin, fur, and feathers.

Cowboy hats have names like the Hispanic, the Real McCoy, Lone Ranger, or the Incredible Green Cowgirl, but none could ever get close to the original "Great Boss of the Plains," made by John B. Stetson on his painful trek west in search of gold.

❚ Stetsons come in different styles: a woven straw stetson (above) and a traditional felt stetson trimmed with a leather band and buttons (top)

The Clamor for Glamor

*T*HE AGGRESSIVE CAPITALISM OF THE 1980S GAVE WAY TO A WORLD directed by more tolerant, liberal, social ideologies. After the Reagan years, Bill Clinton, America's youthful president, was elected on a program for social reform. The end of communism in the Soviet bloc gave Eastern European countries new freedom and hope for democracy and economic growth. Nelson Mandela became South Africa's first black president, ending years of apartheid oppression. Hong Kong returned to China in 1998, and there was hope for solving the Arab-Israeli conflict and bringing peace to the Middle East.

In Britain Thatcherism was considered *passé* and Tony Blair was elected Prime Minister in May 1997, with the promise of a caring, sharing society. France followed by electing a socialist government and the unified Germany voted for Social Democrat Gerhard Schröder in 1998, ending the conservative reign of Helmut Kohl. The European Union expanded to 15 member states and the euro, the new common currency, was born on January 1, 1999.

While Europe was growing the world was shrinking with electronic communications, e-mail, the Internet, and the World Wide Web offering global links within seconds. Inexpensive air travel made the world more accessible and seeing the world became an education for the young and a pleasure for many others.

Eclectic Fashion

The global spirit affected lifestyle, music, dress, and fashion. Many ideological barriers broke down and several taboos and outdated rules in social etiquette disappeared. Diversity of dress conquered

The Supermodels

HATS ON THE CATWALK

Supermodels became icons of beauty and fashion and replaced society beauties and glamorous Hollywood stars of previous decades. Model agencies were forever searching for new faces, fitting the mood of the time and catering for the appetite for rapid change in looks and fashion. From steely Linda Evangelista with her changing hair colors, "Barbie Doll" lookalike Claudia Schiffer, exotic Naomi Campbell or waif-like Kate Moss, they all represented a different post-feminist ideal and were vital for the promotion of fashion products of all kinds.

Nineties catwalk fashion became fantastic and quite remote from the type of clothing women in a modern and egalitarian society required, but it fulfilled a need in the stark, computer-controlled society at the end of the century. Top designer shows in Paris and London became sheer theater, as well as publicity machines in promoting labels and less expensive diffusion lines in accessories, cosmetics, and perfumes. The twice annual fashion trail was still New York, London, Paris, and Milan but fashion designers and their influences became global and their diffusion lines represented very profitable business.

❚ *above left* The waves of the sea translated into hats by Philip Treacy, 1997-98. © Robert Fairer
❚ *above right* A Philip Treacy gold turban made from metallic organza, designed for the 1996-97 collection. © Robert Fairer
❚ *opposite* Glamorous mask hat by Philip Treacy 1998-99: a firework explosion of pink and purple feathers. © Robert Fairer

fashion dictatorship and fitted in with women's busy professional lives, homes, and children. Freedom in fashion did not mean the loss of individuality and accessories played an increasingly important role in the expression of personal style.

An Occasion for Hats?

During the last forty years, hats have not been important enough to call for multi-million-dollar investments, and have remained relatively expensive fashion items. Model hats are shaped and sewn by hand, each representing one or two days' work for an experienced milliner. Even mass-produced hats are hand finished, and factories have not changed their traditional methods of production. Hats have become luxury items and many women have lost the habit of wearing them. Weddings and social occasions of all kinds provide a perfect excuse to buy a beautiful hat and they would be less colorful and fun without them. Whatever the occasion, a hat is the most noticeable and most tribal fashion accessory and needs to reflect the wearer's personality.

Milliners on both sides of the Atlantic have understood this well and are creating hats to suit the mood, occasion, and role of their clients. The millinery profession might be much reduced in size, but it has become more diverse than ever before, creating an eclectic range from woolen caps to theatrical extravaganzas.

A Town Crazy about Hats

London has become a focal point for millinery. The reason for this is the British tradition of honoring special occasions like weddings, royal garden parties, and race meetings, which provide a clientele for traditional millinery businesses as well as opportunities for young designers.

Rediscovering the fun of wearing hats, young people buy witty creations from market stalls to complement their casual dress style. Hair accessories have become the craze, from decorated combs to funky evening hats with feathers and face veils. The signs of a millinery comeback are strong, as young designers emerge all round the world.

Romantic balloon hat by Rachel Skinner created from flower petals and feathers

New York Millinery

The Headwear Information Bureau (HIB) in New York has been in existence since 1989 and runs an annual hat design competition, The Milli Award, with prizes in three categories of headwear: Out of this World, Daytime, and Casual. The award has been developed with the aim of promoting American millinery, a fast-growing industry since the mid-1980s. There have been an estimated $872 million in retail sales in 1999 with a predicted continuous growth of 10-15 percent.

Jan Stanton, of Heartfelt Millinery based in Los Angeles, was awarded the Casual Hat Award in 1999, with her entry of a crushable cloche in Italian ribbed viscose. The hat has a round crown and a narrow brim, turned up softly at the front and trimmed with a neat petersham band and tailored bow. Easy to wear, it has the Heartfelt signature of feminine styles in straw and soft fabrics. Jan also designs small beaded cocktail hats in lace, reminiscent of the 1950s.

Jacqueline Lamont, a graduate from New York's Fashion Institute of Technology, designs hats in her SoHo studio and creates headgear for women with style. Her specialty is using out-of-the-ordinary materials like nylon and leather, snakeskin, patchwork, and camouflage knits. Jacqueline likes to work in an unstructured, soft style, popular for women who don't wear hats every day. "These aren't your grandmother's Sunday bonnets," she says. "A hat should not

1990-2000

1980-1990

1970-1980

1960-1970

1950-1960

1940-1950

1930-1940

1920-1930

1910-1920

1900-1910

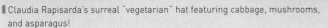

Claudia Rapisarda's surreal "vegetarian" hat featuring cabbage, mushrooms, and asparagus!

Claudia Rapisarda modeling one of her own felt trilbies edged and trimmed with velvet

overpower the wearer, I'm not into fussy ornamentation." Her approach is appreciated by trendsetters like Cindy Crawford and Jodi Foster and some of her hats were included in the Philadelphia Museum of Art's retrospective, *Hats of the 20th Century*.

Also based in a studio in SoHo is Diana Burke, who practices custom-designed traditional millinery combined with modern design. A former partner of Burke-Leggi Fine Millinery, she carries on the same design philosophy with opulent and distinctive creations. Her travels throughout Europe turn up special materials, and frequent visits to antique markets in New England and New York uncover interesting treasures she often puts to use in designing her hat creations. Claudia Rapisarda is another young New York

hatter with all the charismatic enthusiasm of her native Brazil. Claudia has loved hats almost as far back as she can remember and got excited about millinery when she saw for herself the popularity of Carol Denford's Hat Shop in London's Covent Garden in the 1980s. She also loved the swap meet market in San Diego, California, where she started her first millinery enterprise by swapping pizzas for old hats. At home, she lovingly restored the hats and sold them later. Lola Ehrlich in New York gave Claudia's love of hats some direction and taught her traditional millinery techniques after she had graduated from Parson's Fashion Design College in New York.

Dressed in black cropped trousers, lace stockings, and high heels, and wearing one of

her own sexy, black headbands with a very high tuft of burned peacock feathers, and a fitted veil down to her chin, Claudia talks with great passion about hats. She is convinced that hats have a place in future fashion. "Making and creating things traditionally by hand is wonderful and therapeutic in this world of mass production and bonded garments," she says.

Her hat collections are an eclectic expression of colors and styles. Claudia's philosophy is that hats should provide self-expression for the designer as well as the wearer. There are soft felts in pastel colors, small trilbies with jaunty high crowns and feather trimmings, and "vegetarian hats" piled up with artificial fruits, vegetables, and flowers. Her specialty are designs of feather and flower

Hats go into Advertising

T HE ALL-POWERFUL MEDIA LOVES HATS. DESIGNERS ARE WELL AWARE OF
this when they use quite extraordinary, impractical creations
in fashion shows. There may be few repeat orders for extravagant
sculptures adorning the heads of supermodels, but it is always a
good opportunity to get a photo in the fashion magazines or on a
newspaper page. Hats have media power, a fact discovered and
exploited by the advertising industry.

The British company Tilda Rice were among the first to
consider hats for their advertising campaign. The television images
presented were large round plates of carefully arranged food. As the
camera pulled back the plates became hats revealing the faces of
the models, who were performing in a catwalk fashion show.

Paris design house Dior has run a series of pictures in
magazines, advertising lipsticks with the slogan "Diorific" featuring
models in glorious hats which shade their eyes and accentuate
their beautifully-painted lips.

Perrier, the French mineral water company, splashed one of its
distinctive green bottles on a model's head and created an elegant,
spiky hat with the upturned bottle as a trimming on top. The
advertising slogan accompanying the image is simply "In Veaugue."

Max Factor commissioned Philip Treacy to create a hat for a
cosmetics advertising campaign. In true Philip Treacy style, he
created a bright red mask hat with beautiful curves and
proportions, which will always stand out in the flood of beauty
products in international fashion magazines.

Dior used millinery design effectively in their "Diorific" advertising campaign for lipstick and other cosmetics (top); Dolmio made inviting hats from food (center), and Perrier used the image of a mineral water hat to give their product sophisticated fashion appeal (right). Meanwhile, Max Factor sought out the talent of top milliner Philip Treacy to produce this dramatic mask hat to advertise their cosmetic products (opposite)

A spiky-quilled explosion by Rachel Trevor-Morgan. Her witty, stylish approach to millinery first established her name in London in the Eighties

hair decorations attached to headbands, combs, and 12-inch plastic hatpins, which can be simply pushed into a *chignon* to create the extravagant Rapisarda look.

The list of American millinery designers is long and growing. Recognized names include Kokin, James Coviello, Lola, Gila, and British-born Louise Green, who has established one of the most successful highend millinery companies in the United States. She started her business in 1987, after studying art in England, which has given her a fascination for the riches of the past and a passion for ornamentation and color. Ten years later, she was honored with the Millinery Designer of the Year award, sponsored by the Headwear Information Bureau in New York.

A Hatter's Guide to London

The established millinery salons in London— Philip Somerville, Graham Smith, and Frederick Fox—create hats which represent traditional elegance, flattering styles, and fine workmanship. Harrods millinery buyer Tracey Whewell considers classics as essential for her clients, who need the reassurance of timeless chic. She also loves hats by Polish-born Gabriela Ligenza, whose dramatic but very romantic styles were inspired by her architectural background. Arriving in London in the mid-1980s, Gabriela has contributed to the revival of millinery with beautiful, feminine hats— much loved by her London clientele.

Other traditional millinery businesses in London are Peter Bettley, Viv Knowland, and John Boyd. Siggi Millinery is the idea of a young German, Siegfried Hesbacher, who came to Britain with a theater group in 1980. He fell in love with London, produced 12 theatrical cocktail hats for a Notting Hill tailor, and sold all of them to the prestigious Harvey Nichols store.

Herbert Johnson is an address not to be missed. Encouraged by the fashion-conscious Prince of Wales, Johnson started the company one hundred years ago, and the store has been a London tradition ever since. Lock & Co., further down St James's Street, is an even older gentlemen's hatter. They too have recently added a number of women's styles to their range of traditional bowlers, top hats, and panamas.

Gilly Forge joined the millinery band in the early 1980s. Starting up as a law student and journalist in Italy, she came back to London, trained with Frederick Fox, and later opened her own business in 1989. Her beautiful Italian straw hats were featured on many fashion pages, but she is proudest of introducing fake fur hats as a major 1990s trend.

Bailey Tomlin is a design partnership, which has been operating very successfully for over 10 years. Anne Tomlin and Bridget Bailey, with complementary fashion and textile backgrounds, have developed a style of wearable hats with the special touch of original trimmings using fruits, foliage, feathers, and flowers.

Herald & Heart Hatters is the partnership of Tracey Mogard and Ken White. They work out of a charming shop with a workroom above in South London. International fame arrived with the film *Four Weddings and a Funeral* and Andie McDowell wearing the famous, much-photographed black straw hat. The hat made her the star of the film from the beginning, and is a perfect example of the decisive power a hat can have as an accessory. "There were other very beautiful hats in the film," says Tracey modestly. "Our black straw hat was picked as one of many by Lindy Hemmings, the costume designer for the film." Herald & Heart Hatters did not think any more about it all, until a phone call from Los Angeles six months later announced that the hat had won a fashion magazine's Accessory of the Year award. This stylish, black, wide-brimmed hat opened a pathway to the American stores and Tracey is still getting repeat orders.

Herald & Heart Hatters are feeling very positive about the future. "We have a captive clientele here in Britain, the summer season with races and weddings provides plenty of work for milliners," Tracey confidently believes. Younger women love wearing more outrageous styles and she is convinced that men will rediscover hats, too. Ken started a line of imported men's felt hats from Poland, and Herald & Heart Hatters are also the UK agent for Stetson in the United States.

A Soft Look

Soft, casual fabric hats were pioneered and first worn by young fashion students during the 1980s. The new casual headgear was rejected by established milliners as "not hats at all" but it filled a gap in the hat market. Made from velvet, leather, and many other fabrics, the soft hats were fun to wear, easy to look after, and not as precious and expensive as stiffly-constructed model hats.

Fred Bare may seem like a strange name for a hat company. The designers behind the business, Carolyn Brookes-Davies and Anita Evagora, are two graduates from the Royal College of Art who set up business in 1983. They were so poor that they felt as "thread bare" as worn fabric and the name for their company was born. Carolyn and Anita had been sculpture and ceramics students and originally thought of making hats to finance their art. They had no millinery training and "invented" their first beret by drawing a circle around a plate. With youthful boldness, as they both admit, they put on a hat each and took more in a bag along London's King's Road trying to find a shop which would sell them. They did not have to go far. A woman passing by asked them about the hats they were wearing, looked in the bag and bought the whole contents for cash on the spot.

The next courageous move was to set up shop far away from the fashion scene, in

1990–2000

1980–1990

1970–1980

1960–1970

1950–1960

1940–1950

1930–1940

1920–1930

1910–1920

1900–1910

▌*top* Gabriela Ligenza's black **synamay** straw and silk organza hat

▌*above* Dramatic red marguerites on a straw cloche by Herald and Heart Hatters

▌ Bailey Tomlin, a millinery design team formed in the late Eighties, specializes in beautiful, easy-to-wear straw hats with ruched, draped, and ruffled fabric trimmings

Eric Javits

PRACTICAL SCULPTURES

Packable styles are a specialty of Eric Javits in New York, America's premier hat designer with branches in Los Angeles, Dallas, and Atlanta. He offers a whole range of "packable hats" in linen, cotton, velvet, and soft chenille. Javits' most original invention is his Wig Hat Collection, which he calls: "The easy, fast, low-maintenance solution, always looking good, whether on the beach or in the city." A band of synthetic hair is attached with velcro to the inside of the hat and can transform the wearer's image in seconds. The falls can be ordered in five different hair colors and are ideal for concealing post-operative cosmetic surgery lines as well as a welcome solution for women suffering hair loss after chemotherapy.

Eric Javits is described as a designer who celebrates women and sees hats as sculptures for the face. After graduating from Rhode Island School of Design in 1978, he discovered how various forms could flatter and alter the face. Millinery seemed a perfect medium for combining his interests: fashion and art. He never looked back and built a multimillion-dollar business, producing over 100,000 hats a year. Voted three times Hat Designer of the Year by the Millinery Institute of America, he is a member of the prestigious Council of Fashion Designers of America.

As well as packable hats, which have been an enormous hit with women in the United States, as well as in Europe and Japan, Eric Javits creates a wide range of model hats, individually hand-painted straws, soft fox fur hats, and airy, pastel pink organza cloches. His hats are available in Neiman Marcus and Saks Fifth Avenue and have crowned famous celebrities, like Whitney Houston, Diane Keaton, and Ivana Trump. The First Lady, Hillary Clinton, wore an Eric Javits hat for Princess Diana's funeral. Madeleine Albright chose a Javits "Squishee" hat, a light, casual, packable straw which must have been just the right hat for her busy life and travels around the world.

❙ Soft feminine American styles inspired by Eric Javits: (clockwise from top left) Javits shows his packable street style in this small woven cloche hat; luxurious glamor is conveyed in his design of a red fox fur hat framing the face; Javits' romantic deep tiffany cloche in pink crinoline and silk organza trimmed with roses; large casual off-the-face sou'wester-style in natural straw

Patricia Underwood

ELEGANT SIMPLICITY

Most famous for her timeless exquisite hats is Patricia Underwood, a milliner of refined simplicity, working in New York. Her hats are recognizable by their utterly plain styles, which just ease into shape on the wearer's head. Adapting the traditional Florentine technique of sewing fine straw plaits into spiral forms, she uses the same process with fine leather strips and felt for flexible shapes and styles. Cashmere is the finest and latest addition to the range of materials. Decoration doesn't exist for Patricia Underwood's hats as her designs rely on shape, color, and proportion, instead of fancy trimmings of feathers and flowers.

Underwood's fascination with millinery was discovering the possibilities hats could create and the different messages styles can convey about the wearer. Patricia Underwood's hats are instantly recognizable and are trusted investments for fashion-conscious women with a love of sleek elegance. She has collaborated with some of America's most prestigious designers including Bill Blass, Donna Karan, Calvin Klein, and Marc Jacobs. Her company is committed to manufacture all the orders in America, which might be the reason for her lasting and uncopied styles. In recognition of her outstanding work she has received a Coty award, a CFDA award, and an American Accessories Achievement award.

As for the future of millinery, she stated in an interview with London's *Financial Times* in 1994: "Today there is a new young generation which does not associate hats with churchgoing or eccentric aunts or grandmothers. They are discovering and, in some cases, rediscovering, themselves in hats."

▎*above* Chocolate brown felt cloche by Patricia Underwood, characterised by an elegant, refined simplicity of style and quality of craftsmanship that requires hours of refinement

▎*opposite* Underwood became a milliner on an impulse decision made during the late Seventies. She quickly established her new approach to headwear, designing plain, pliable shapes by machine-stitching leather strips to make hats like this black trilby

▌A striking cocktail hat extravaganza of black lacquered feather quills by Rachel Trevor-Morgan

▌Millinery as art—delicate feather quill constructions by Dai Rees

London's East End, on a street that doubles as a flower market on Sundays. Opening only on Sundays, this hat salon with a difference was original and fun and attracted London's gardeners as well as fashion-conscious trendies from all over town.

Easy to wear, inexpensive, and fun Fred Bare hats became a craze in London. Next, a new and fashionable retail chain liked the styles and gave Anita and Carolyn an order for 3,000 hats, paid for in advance. This overnight success was quite a shock and they had to find a factory for production. Success and recognition led inevitably to the pirating of designs, but such is life and the hat trade is renowned for "borrowing" each other's ideas.

Further pioneers from the 1980s are Carol and Nigel Denford who created The Hat Shop in London's Covent Garden after starting with a market stall. The couple offered customers an eclectic mix of hats, and the shop was the talk of London. Queues formed outside on Saturdays, extraordinary for normally quiet hat businesses, and manufacturers from Luton who were proclaiming "the end of the hat trade" came to London just to see this spectacle.

Sandra Phillipps is a fashion design graduate who specialized in millinery, selling hats to Harrods while she was still at college. She established a successful company in Tunbridge Wells, south of London. Setting up a hat business out of London was a risk, but it paid off, and the company now has a staff of 10, plus about 30 outside workers.

The Young Avant-Garde in Millinery

Leading international modern millinery in London are hat designers Stephen Jones and Philip Treacy. The strength of their design ideas and their work with high profile fashion designers has generated publicity—and stunning hats. Both are to be credited with lifting millinery into a new age and have become leaders for established milliners and an inspiration to the next generation of young hatmakers.

Dai Rees, the latest discovery in the world of catwalk shows, might soon complete the triumvirate. A graduate in ceramics from the Royal College of Art, the young Welshman has impressed the fashion media with his

unusual approach to hats. Dai literally found his fame and possibly fortune on a gray afternoon when, unemployed and depressed, he took a walk in the park. The geese on the pond had been molting and the ground was littered with feathers. Thinking they were quite beautiful, Dai picked the feathers up and took them home to experiment with. It amused him to construct things from these "treasures," which should have ended up in the park's garbage collection.

Dai's neighbor happened to be Katy England, who was working for fashion designer Alexander McQueen. She suggested that Dai should show his quill constructions to McQueen, who ordered 50 pieces on the spot to accessorize his 1997 Spring/Summer collection. The success of these "delicate cages" was phenomenal; within two years, a team of six was working on orders, supplying 26 stockists around the world.

Today Dai has adapted his ideas to a full range of wearable hats. He plans to expand into other accessories but for now his hopes are to find a new clientele for hats and reinvent the notion of the "cocktail hat." Unlike Dai, Prudence is a designer with a

▌Feathered turban with corkscrew top by Rachel Skinner

1990–2000

1980–1990

1970–1980

1960–1970

1950–1960

1940–1950

1930–1940

1920–1930

1910–1920

1900–1910

passion for traditional millinery, who loves making things "in an old fashioned way." "My hats could be made in 1899 as well as 1999," she says. "I love doing beautiful things by hand." It was this love of perfect craftsmanship that led to her making hats for Vivienne Westwood's collections twice a year.

As a designer, Vivienne Westwood is well known for her appreciation of traditionally crafted garments. Prudence saw an Eighties television interview with Vivienne, in which she talked about her tailor and how much she liked being surrounded by people with traditional skills. This struck a chord, and Prudence contacted Vivienne to offer her services as a milliner. The offer was accepted and the collaboration has been mutually beneficial ever since.

Known only as "Prudence," she hails from Princetown, New Jersey but studied millinery privately for seven years with Rose Cory in London. Traditional skills take a long time to perfect, which is the reason for model hats being so expensive. Too expensive, according to Prudence, which is one of the problems. "There is no room for beautiful hats on a limited budget," she says, "and there is not enough choice. Furthermore, a hat belongs to a way of dressing that young women of today have not been taught by their mothers," she says with regret. "You can see it by watching them pick hats up by their brims, like bicycle wheels!"

Jo Gordon and Pip Hackett are young rising stars, graduating from the Royal College of Art, Britain's regular supplier of new talent. Wendy Dagworthy of the RCA says that only one or two places are offered every year on the specialist millinery postgraduate course. On the question about the future of hats, she is extremely confident and optimistic. "It is important to understand that there was a non-hat-wearing age before and I am positive that there will be a hat-wearing age again."

Unusually, Nicola de Selincourt and Lou Garside are young designers without arts backgrounds. They gave up careers in music and advertising to start hat salons, catering for an exclusive young clientele in London's South Kensington. Starting out at evening classes in millinery they gradually became hooked on hatmaking as a career.

 Twin horns draped in soft leather by Pip Hackett

∥ Marie Mercié's giant spider eyeing a butterfly perched on its web

Milliners of Belgium and Holland

Across the English Channel, in Belgium, a young hatter of Italian ancestry by the name of Elvis Pompilio has created waves of excitement in Paris and London. Pompilio started making hats in the mid-1980s and opened his first showroom in Brussels, Belgium, in 1987. This was followed by two shops in Antwerp, Belgium, and the acquisition of a former hat factory, which he transformed into a studio. The address he chose for his business was delightfully

appropriate—Rue du Chapeau or Hat Street. What makes Elvis Pompilio so special are his colorful creations, combined with his modern outlook in making hats for men and women. Working with internationally-acclaimed fashion designers like Ann Demeulemeester and Louis Féraud, he accessorizes their twice-yearly fashion shows. A diffusion line of his products is available in outlets around the world.

Farther east in Holland is a millinery business created by Berry Rutjes Jr. Discovering hats several years ago, she installed a hat shop in her parent's hotel

in Gouda, and offers intensive millinery courses for clients from Germany, Belgium, and Holland.

Parisian Chapeaux

In Paris, only a fraction of the former millinery glory remains, but an interest in *la mode des chapeaux* is growing among young people. The name in Parisian hatmaking is Marie Mercié, who works with originality and a touch of modernism. She feels passionately that the *grisaille* (grayness) in fashion is coming to an end and that women want to laugh, have fun, and dress colorfully again. Marie calls this *feminité baroque,* which is already expressing itself with the revival of fancy, feminine lingerie.

Charming, relaxed, and ever so slightly eccentric, Marie Mercié wears jodhpurs, a riding jacket, and hat with the kind of *chic* unique to Parisian women. Fashion magazines praised her for rescuing the hat from the confines of church services and weddings. She states: "Hats are the eccentrics of the fashion world, and important because they are worn close to the brain."

Her millinery career started relatively late, when she married English art critic Tony Peto, who encouraged her to channel her boundless energies into hats. After a protected childhood in Fontainbleau, near Paris, she studied archaeology and history of art before joining a French TV station in 1968, as a TV scriptwriter.

Her first shop in the Rue Tiquetonne was like a tiny pink box bursting with hats and was followed by a more spacious one, Rue St-Sulpice, on the left bank of the Seine, which is her main shop today.

Philippe Model has his business across the river Seine in the Marché St-Honoré which is a more traditional area for millinery in Paris. His Boutique Chapeau is designed like a ship, with gray hatstands and portholes. The lower level, referred to as

Elvis Pompilio, the mad hatter of Belgium, surrounded by his designs

Parisian chic gigantic straw, smothered in white silk organza and trimmed with silk flowers, by Marie Mercié

la piscine, is a four-sided display of bridal accessories. The illuminated, heavy glass shelves give the impression of water and space, a swimming pool with hats floating on the edges.

Originally from Sens, less than 100 miles from Paris, Phillipe Model has also set up his hat production there. Starting out in 1978 he learned his trade from the great master of French millinery, Jean Barthet. When his hat shop was opened in 1984, it became a focal point for chic women from all over the world, choosing hats for the *Prix de Diane* in Chantilly, a horserace meeting and society event in the French summer season.

Jean Barthet and Jean-Charles Brosseau, the masters of the 1960s and 70s, are still making hats. Jean Barthet designs only for a select private clientele, while Jean-Charles Brosseau manages his new exciting shop located under former railway arches near the Gare de Lyon in association with his son.

Josette Denus, of the same generation, still works actively in her salon opened in 1984. After a 30-year association with Paulette, whom she joined as an 15-year-old apprentice, she runs her business on the traditions of *haute mode* (*couture* millinery). With years of experience behind her, Josette's

spirit, love, and enthusiasm for her work is undiminished. She believes in impeccable workmanship and poses hats on her clients' heads in front of a three-angled mirror. "Before being creative, it is essential to respect fundamental techniques of construction. It's like building a house, putting the curtains up at the end is easy." Her devoted clientele includes *haute couture* houses, society women, and French aristocracy. Sometimes whole families comes to be "hatted" for a wedding.

La Maison Michel in the Rue Ste-Anne still stands as a focal point for the Paris millinery world, as well as for designers from Britain and the United States. This was its mission when the company was created in the 1940s and it still provides a link for young designers as well as conserving the traditions of the past.

Heritage of Hats

Hats have played a vital role in the history of fashion, and the story of millinery on both sides of the Atlantic is full of fascinating facts and stories. The rich heritage and social changes are historically fascinating and of great value for young hatmakers of the future.

1990–2000
1980–1990
1970–1980
1960–1970
1950–1960
1940–1950
1930–1940
1920–1930
1910–1920
1900–1910

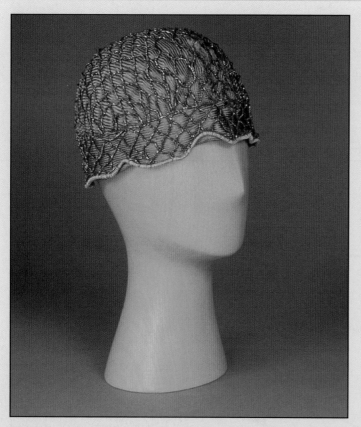

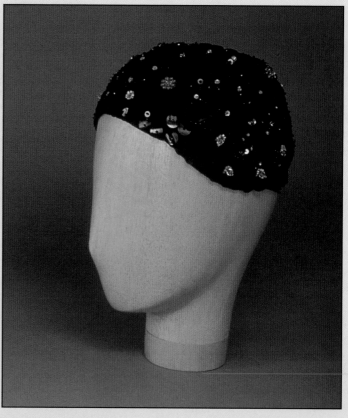

▮ Evening cloche hat (1925) made in blue silk and embroidered with metallic pearls (left). Black evening cap by Jeanne Lanvin (1925), made from silk velvet covered with shiny black sequins and pearls (right). Both hats are from the collection of the Musée du Chapeau, Chazelles-sur-Lyon, France

▮ Parisian design of the 1940s: a soft fur felt style trimmed with veilings and feathers from the collection of the Musée du Chapeau, Chazelles-sur-Lyon, France

The Philadelphia Museum of Art houses an important collection of over 400 hats, which, according to Anne d'Harnoncourt, the George D. Widener Director at the museum, are an expression of twentieth-century woman and provide a vivid picture of social changes and cross-cultural influences. The millinery items preserved range from a sober black velvet riding hat dated 1740 to a bright blue, space helmet style by Pierre Cardin, designed in 1968, celebrating the American landing on the moon. A shocking pink "free-form satin wave" by Givenchy dates from 1988 and there are examples of work by young milliners of the 1990s, creating hats for the end of the century.

In a special hat exhibition in 1993 called *Ahead of Fashion*, Dilys E. Blum, the curator of the Costume and Textiles Department, presented a mix of history, humor, and elegance with an array of twentieth century women's hats. Included in the display were creations by famous French milliners, like Reboux, Agnès, and Paulette in the first half

1990–2000

1980–1990

1970–1980

1960–1970

1950–1960

1940–1950

1930–1940

1920–1930

1910–1920

1900–1910

of this century. Other exhibits had made history: the lace bonnet Grace Kelly wore at her wedding to Prince Rainier in 1956 and surreal designs by Franco-Italian designer Schiaparelli. Top American milliner Lilly Daché was represented by a charismatic, rose-trimmed, wool felt hat with divided flaps at the back, inspired by caps worn by the French Foreign Legion. Mr John of New York was remembered for his exquisite, jewelled snake cocktail hat

In the south of France, in Chazelles-sur-Lyon, is the Musée du Chapeau which exhibits not only hats, but also materials, blocks, and machinery, all arranged to explain to the visitor the art and craft of hatmaking. Driven by her love of hats and her belief in the preservation of the past, Eliane Bolomier, the curator at Chazelles, offers visits with demonstrations, special exhibitions, and the membership of a hatlovers' club. Founded in the 1980s, *Club Chapeau Passion* has 140 members from all over the world. Regular newsletters provide information about the past and the present of the hat industry and form a vital link for all hat enthusiasts.

The museum harks back to a thriving hat industry in the 1930s, when 2,200 people worked as hatters in this small town in the Lyonnais mountains.

The origins of felt and hatmaking date back to the sixteenth century, when it is said that *chevaliers* (knights) from Malta imported camel fur from the Middle East. Chazelles-sur-Lyon became one of the most important hat-producing centers in the world; well known for its finest quality felt hats. The internationally famous company, *La Maison Fléchet*, founded in 1859, had a large factory, employing 600 workers in its 1930s hey-day. The business stayed in the same family until its closure in 1976, a casualty to the general decline in hat-wearing. Today, the vast factory buildings are a reminder of a prosperous past and the hat museum with its wealth of information preserves the memory of its workforce.

The county of Bedfordshire, England has been home to the straw hat industry for the past 300 years. Historical accounts from 1689 tell of 14,000 people earning their living solely by making straw hats. The town of

❚ Luton in Bedfordshire, England, was historically the center of straw plaiting and a town renowned for its hatters. Even the local police force, founded in 1876 and consisting of 12 men, were fitted with straw helmets

Luton was the center of the industry and its museum houses archives and a historical collection of hats. The Luton Museum Service also offers a hat trail which leads the visitor along 43 points of historical and cultural interest such as small factories, warehouses, and the occasional pub with names like The Mad Hatter Club.

Boon & Lane Blockmakers, in the heart of the town, are a unique and indispensable establishment for milliners and hat manufacturers. Mr Boon and Mr Lane make their living carving wooden blocks, copies of designer shapes, to be sent all over the world. Blockmaking is a special skill, requiring craftsmanship and an eye for the finest details of a hat's line and style. Boon & Lane also produce metal pans for use in mass-production hat factories. Often copies of

wooden blocks, these are carved in plaster, before being cast in metal.

Two hundred miles further north is Stockport, south of Manchester; another key hat industry area of the past. Since its founding in 1773, the company Christy & Co. Headwear dominated the town, producing men's felt hats and the well-recognized British policeman's helmet made from finest navy blue fur felt. However, Christy & Co. Ltd has also fallen victim to the changing times of hatwearing, but Stockport is celebrating its heritage with Hat Works—the Museum of the Hatting Industry. The unique collection of hatmaking machinery and tools will provide visitors to the museum with a nostalgic encounter with a millinery past and may hopefully inspire a future generation of hatmakers and hatwearers.

Philip Treacy

A Touch of Celtic Brilliance

Irish-born hat stylist Philip Treacy's shop in London's elegant Belgravia is an Aladdin's cave of fashion accessories. Gold walls are set off by ornate mirrors and futuristic chairs shaped like golden lilies. Chunky shelves are laden with items any woman might dream of buying. There are stylish leather handbags, precious satin evening bags, luxurious devoré scarves in soft, warm colors, and smooth leather gloves with fur cuffs. Presiding over it all are the unmistakable Philip Treacy hats. Some are displayed on tall perspex stands and surreal female mannequins, some are perched on top of expensive handbags, and others—elegant and self-assured—are simply placed about the store, confident in the knowledge that they have all been designed by the 1990s' undisputed master of millinery design.

An American client chooses a scarf and other items which are packed in blue boxes with gold ribbons and bows. At the back of the shop, Philip Treacy, tall, blond, and lanky, is dealing with a buyer from Germany about the next collection, and around him friendly young assistants make sure that everybody is happy. Mr Pig, Philip's much-photographed little dog, makes a round of the store full of purpose and authority, and, satisfied that all is in order, jumps back into his basket.

Like Philip Treacy's designs, the atmosphere in his shop is exciting and glamorous, but not at all pretentious or fussy. His vision of fashion is egalitarian. "Glamor will always be desirable and need not be elitist, glamor and fashion should be for everyone," he says. This statement may not seem quite in keeping with his luxurious, expensive, and extraordinary designs, but Philip Treacy is totally convincing when he explains in his soft Irish accent: "I have the opportunity to say something with hats. I am interested in capturing people's imagination, even if one has to shout louder than before." He might well be right, millinery design needs strong statements after decades of decline.

Philip Treacy was born in Galway on Ireland's west coast in 1967. One of eight children, his upbringing was hardly luxurious, but he has talked of his background as a "safety net." This, and not having encountered fashion until he was 18 years old, might well be the reason for his remaining so down-to-earth.

He studied fashion design in Dublin, and won a scholarship to continue his studies at London's Royal College of Art, graduating in 1990. The following year, he opened his first showroom. It hardly seems possible that his meteoric rise to fame and everything that has happened since could have been squeezed into a time frame of just a few years.

Catwalk shows take up his time, as well as managing his growing business. Philip Treacy has created hats for several top designers in Paris and it was Karl Lagerfeld who was the first to discover the power of Treacy's hats in a fashion show. Others like John Galliano, Rifat Ozbek, and Valentino soon followed.

In 1993, Philip Treacy staged a fantastic millinery show in which top supermodels paraded his wonderful creations. The show made headlines the following day, putting hats and millinery firmly back center stage in fashion and, most importantly, in the minds of millions of people, who had lost touch with hats during the three decades before. Worldwide media coverage of Philip Treacy's work continues, and his name has become closely identified with millinery for hat lovers, as well as for those indifferent to hat wearing.

Winning the British Accessory Designer of the Year award for the first time in 1991, at the very start of his career, Philip Treacy has won the award five times more. A diffusion line for major British department stores has made Philip Treacy hats available to a wider public. In 1997, he launched an accessories line, including handbags, scarves, gloves, and hair ornaments. A dedicated workaholic, who thrives on the demands of his business, Philip Treacy is also a committed craftsman, who believes that design must be backed by perfect workmanship.

Philip Treacy's vision for the future includes raising people's perception of glamor through his hat creations. He would like to replace conformist accessories of past decades and create "rebellious" ones in their place. "The Sixties did away with hats, because people wanted hair. The reverse might well happen in the future. I will keep on showing people interesting hats and something may 'click,' then they will see them in a new light. The reason for wearing a hat should not be convention, but only to make a woman feel good."

Reluctant to be drawn into more predictions about hats and the future, he muses, "I love the unknown, who knows what will happen? The nature of fashion is change." Asked how casual street styles could relate to his glamorous vision of fashion, he replies, "Everyday casual sportswear is not the be all and end all. There is always interest in glamor which will affect the future. The catwalk is the melting pot of ideas, they filter down. It has always been like that, the only difference is they filter down faster than before with ever increasing speed, for diffusion worldwide. I want to change the shortsighted idea that hats are old fashioned."

With his drive, determination, and powers of persuasion, Philip Treacy will take up the challenge, well into the new century.

opposite Unmistakably Philip Treacy: an explosion in red and white feathers for his 1998-99 spring collection. © Robert Fairer

far left Another witty feather creation framing the face in orange and black, from the 1998-99 collection. © Robert Fairer

center Refined sophisticated wit—a delicate cocktail hat with a shower of white feathers. © Robert Fairer

below A commanding millinery design of the 1996-97 collection in red, one of Treacy's favorite colors. © Robert Fairer

Glossary

aigrette a feather trimming

bandeau a band forming a hat fitting; a narrow band worn round the head to hold the hair in position

beret a round, flattish cap of felt or cloth

bicorn hat with brim turned up on two sides

block hat mold made from wood or metal used for shaping material into a hat

blocking cords a strong cord to secure materials to the wooden hat blocks

boater a flat-topped, hardened straw hat with a flat brim

bonnet a woman or child's hat tied under the chin, typically with a brim framing the face

bowler a man's hard felt hat with round, dome-shaped crown

breton hat with brim turned up evenly all around; derived from national dress in Brittany, France (**half-breton** a brim turned up at the front only)

brim the projecting edge around the bottom of a hat

canotier French word for sailor or boater

capeline flat wide brim; preshaped felt or straw raw material for hat making

chapeau mou soft, squashable hat or turban

chapelier the French word for hat maker

chéchia cylindrical cap worn by men in northern Africa

cheerer nineteenth-century men's felt hat with flat crown

cloche bell-shaped, brimmed hat made famous in the 1920s

conformateur device for measuring and mapping the shape of a person's head

coolie a broad conical hat made in one piece with a pointed crown, worn by laborers in some Asian countries

crinoline a synthetic material which replaced crin made from horsehair. Used for stiffening materials as a foundation and for trimmings

cossack hat a tall, cylindrical Russian hat, fluted upwards and outwards

crown the top of a hat

deerstalker a soft cloth cap, originally worn for hunting, with peaks in front and behind, and earflaps which can be tied together on top of the head or under the chin

faille fine ribbed silk fabric

fedora a man's soft felt hat with a curled brim and low crown dented lengthwise

felt bonded material for hats made by rolling and compressing wool or other animal hair

fez a flat-topped, conical hat formerly the Turkish national headdress

headband inside fitting for a hat, usually made from petersham ribbon

Homburg a man's hard felt hat with slightly dented crown and narrow curled brim, named after the town in Germany

hood preshaped material for hatmaking; can be straw or felt

modiste the French word for milliner

moiré silk fabric with embossed watermarks forming a marbled pattern

mushroom cloche cloche with rounded, down-curved brim

nutria finest beaver fur of a soft brown color

pan metal block used for mass production of hats

panama man's wide-brimmed, fine-woven straw hat from Equador, shipped through Panama

petersham ribbed fabric or ribbon (French *gros-grain*) used for headbands, bindings, and trimmings

picture hat large brimmed and elaborately trimmed hat

pillbox small, box shaped hat made famous by Jackie Kennedy

plumassier the French word for feathermaker

profile asymmetrical shape hiding one side of the face

postillion eighteenth-century ladies' riding hat with flat crown and slightly curled brim

shellac a mercury based stiffener for felt, used in the nineteenth century to perfect a bowler hat

silk beaver hat the finest man's top hat

skylarker small hat, shaped forwards, derived from the skylark bird with a tuft on its head

slouch hat soft brimmed felt hat made famous by Greta Garbo

smoking cap or hat man's velvet cap with tassel, designed to keep the cigar smells from the hair

snood a crocheted or knotted net to keep the hair in place at the back of the head

sou'wester a waterproof hat with a broad brim

sparterie/esparterie a stiff woven material used in high class millinery as a foundation to be covered, as well as for block making, i.e. sparterie blocks

spartalac thick white stiffener for sparterie blocks

stetson a hat with a high crown and wide brim, traditionally worn by cowboys and ranchers in the United States

stiffening felt, straw, or gelatin stiffeners are generally used to reinforce fabrics in hatmaking

sweatband a band of absorbant material to soak up sweat and keep hair from the face, often used by sportspeople; a band of absorbant material lining a hat

synamay a lightweight, transparent woven straw fabric

top hat/topper man's formal hat with high cylindrical crown, traditionally black or gray

toque high cylindrical cap, worn deep over the forehead

tricorn a brimmed hat turned up on three sides

trilby man's felt hat with narrow brim and indented crown

trimmings decorations used for hats e.g. bands, bows

turban a draped hat, inspired by Muslim and Sikh headdresses, consisting of a long length of cotton or silk wound round a cap or the head

Bibliography

The Feminine Ideal
Marianne Thesander
Reaktion Books Ltd (1997)

Chanel–the Couturière at Work
Amy de la Haye and Shelley Tobin
The Victoria and Albert Museum,
London (1994)

Gloria Swanson
Richard Hudson and Raymond Lee
Castle Books, New York (1970)

The Man in the Bowler Hat
Fred Miller Robinson
The University of North Carolina
Press,
Chapel Hill and London (1993)

Patou
Meredith Etherington-Smith
St Martin's/Marek
Hutchinson & Co., London (1983)

Authentic French Fashions of the Twenties
JoAnne Olian
Dover Publications, Inc., New York
(1990)

Undressing the Cinema
Stella Bruzzi
Routledge, London (1997)

Trilby
George du Maurier
Everyman, J.M. Dent, London (1931)

The Art of Vogue Covers 1909-1940
William Packer
Octopus Books Ltd, London (1980)

Hats in Vogue since 1910
Christina Probert
Thames and Hudson Ltd, London
© Condé Nast (1981)

In Vogue, Six Decades of Fashion
Edited by Georgina Howell
Allen Lane, London
© Condé Nast (1975)

Lanvin, Fashion Memoir
Elisabeth Barillé
Thames and Hudson Ltd, London
(1997)

Le Siècle en Chapeaux, Claude Saint-Cyr
Jacqueline Demorex
Edition du May, Paris (1991)

Elsa Schiaparelli, Empress of Paris Fashion
Palmer White
Aurum Press Ltd, London (1995)

Die Hüte der Adele List
Gerda Buxbaum
Prestel Verlag, Munchen-New York
(1995)

Garbo
Norman Zierold
W. H. Allen & Co., Ltd (1970)

Magic Names of Fashion
Ernestine Carter
Weidenfeld and Nicolson, London
(1980)

Le Béret
Philippe Jouvion
Editions du Rouergue, France (1998)

Heads and Tales
Aage Thaarup
Cassell & Company Ltd, London
(1956)

Christian Dior
Diana de Marly
B.T. Batsford Ltd, London (1990)

Yves Saint Laurent
Pierre Bergé
Thames and Hudson Ltd, London
(1997)

The Cowboy Hat
William Reynolds and Ritch Rand
Gibbs and Smith, Layton Utah 84041,
USA (1995)

Stetson Hats
Jeffrey B. Snyder
Schiffer Publishing (1997)

Panama: A Legendary Hat
by Martine Buchet
Editions Assouline

Clothes
James Laver
Burke Publishing, London (1952)

Index